"*Global Wealth, Local Impact* is one of those rare business books that manages to be both intellectually rigorous and genuinely human. Stephanie Forbes does not treat supply chains as abstract systems or technical afterthoughts; she treats them as living architectures of power, trust, risk, and consequence. That framing alone sets this book apart.

"What struck me most is how seamlessly Forbes moves between centuries—Roman grain logistics, Silk Road relationships, East India Company negotiations—and today's boardroom realities without ever losing relevance or credibility. These are not historical anecdotes used for color; they are analytical mirrors. Each one forces the reader to confront a simple but uncomfortable truth: volatility, disruption, and imbalance are not modern failures—they are recurring conditions, and leadership is defined by how deliberately we design for them.

"The chapters on negotiation, partnership governance, and risk sharing are particularly sharp. Forbes dismantles the myth that 'efficiency' alone creates resilience and replaces it with a far more mature argument: resilience is built through structure, transparency, and disciplined relationships. Her treatment of governance—not as bureaucracy, but as an enabler of trust and speed—will resonate deeply with leaders who have lived through partnerships that looked good on paper and quietly failed in practice.

"Equally compelling is the book's refusal to separate economic performance from ethical consequence. Without being preachy, *Global Wealth, Local Impact* makes clear that value chains do not just move goods; they shape communities, labor conditions, financial stability, and national outcomes. That perspective is long overdue.

"This is not a book you skim for tactics. It is a book you return to— because it sharpens how you think, not just what you do. Forbes has written a playbook for leaders who understand that the future belongs not to those chasing optimization, but to those building systems strong enough—and honest enough—to endure."

> **—DR. CHIKA C. DANIELS,** PhD., MRAIC, NOMA, RIBA, president and chief visionary of WTAL Canada and member of the Executive Council, Office of the Premier of Alberta

"Most business books talk about supply chains from a distance. *Global Wealth, Local Impact* meets them where they actually live: at the intersection of governance, negotiation, execution, and risk. Stephanie Forbes does not romanticize complexity. She explains it, respects it, and gives leaders and practitioners a clear framework for navigating it. This is a rare book that speaks equally to executives shaping strategy and professionals carrying the weight of delivery. It is smart, grounded, and deeply relevant to how modern organizations function."

> **— ANTON J. GUNN,** chairman of the Columbia Metropolitan Airport Commission

"Amid constant disruption, *Global Wealth, Local Impact* offers the clarity and strategic grounding business leaders urgently need. Stephanie Forbes' wealth of experience connects the dots between history, global dynamics, and everyday decisions, making this essential reading regardless of your industry or title. It's rare to find a book with this scope, and it serves as a guide for anyone looking to sharpen their game plan and unlock meaningful growth."

> **—CATHERINE LANG-CLINE,** award-winning CEO and author of *The Rules of the Game for Women in Business*

"*Global Wealth, Local Impact* is a practical and timely supply chain management playbook for leaders navigating an increasingly volatile and interconnected world. Stephanie Forbes translates complex global supply chain dynamics into clear, actionable strategy, guiding readers through historical insight, operational discipline, and real-world application.

"With a strong focus on building resilient supply chains, mastering negotiation, and driving cooperative growth through partnerships and alliances, Forbes addresses inflationary pressure and economic uncertainty with agility and precision. She brings clarity to what truly matters in modern supply chains, what to measure, how to govern, and how to prepare for global events that test resilience equipping leaders to shape future value chains and deliver durable results in a rapidly shifting global landscape."

> **—DESIREE BOMBENON,** MBA, ICD.D, purpose-driven social entrepreneur, Queen Elizabeth II Platinum Jubilee Medal recipient, Top 100 Most Powerful Women Hall of Fame leader, and CEO of aspiHer Premier Women's Business Club

"Stephanie Forbes writes as I heard her speak for decades - with passion, perspective, and remarkable wit.

"This is truly a value chain playbook, grounded by historical ways and means invented by: the Roman Empire's 'Appian Way,' sourcing hungry sharks and minting silver coins; the Silk Road, as she argues was the 'world's original LinkedIn' and 'first information superhighway'; and those commodity trading/commercial inventions mastered by the East India Company.

"Stephanie ties past wonders of the ancient commercial world with modern-day supply chain challenges, drivers, and advanced intelligence/AI tools. With world-class examples that inspire, she guides the reader in search of new value chains to solve local and global trade disruption. It will re-ignite their careers and help make a difference in their chosen playing field."

—**WILLIAM (BILL) SYKES,** data everything advisor at Cascadia Projects Inc. and retired partner at Ernst & Young Consulting, Critical Technologies

"*Global Wealth, Local Impact* is a masterclass in turning complexity into clarity. Stephanie Forbes blends history, strategy, and actionable insights to show how supply chains aren't just operational necessities, they're engines of resilience, innovation, and global prosperity. This book is essential reading for leaders who want to future-proof their organizations and create value that lasts."

—**HON. LEELA SHARON AHEER ECA,** former minister, deputy leader and MLA, and founder and CEO of Slam Industries Inc.

"Stephanie Forbes has written a timely and highly practical guide for anyone working within today's complex value chains. *Global Wealth, Local Impact* translates complexity into clear, usable insight, bridging strategy and on-the-ground execution in a way that benefits both senior leaders and professionals in the trenches. This is a book that will resonate across industries and geographies."

—**CATHERINE BROWNLEE,** president of CBI Business Solutions

"As the founder of Resilient New Media Inc., I spend my days helping thought leaders and entrepreneurs build systems that can actually support growth, not just creativity. *Global Wealth, Local Impact* is one of those rare books that changes how you see your business from the inside out.

"Stephanie Forbes makes it clear that success isn't just about having a great product or service, it's about understanding the entire value chain that supports it. For a small agency, this book is a wake-up call and a road map. It shows how partnerships, negotiations, operations, and even contingency planning are not 'big company problems,' but essential disciplines for any business that wants to scale sustainably.

"What I value most is how practical the lessons are. Even a lean team can apply the principles in this book to strengthen vendor relationships, reduce risk, improve margins, and make smarter strategic decisions. You don't need a global operation to think globally, you need clarity, structure, and intention.

"If you run a small agency and want to move from reactive growth to resilient growth, this book will fundamentally improve how you build, protect, and expand your business."

—KIM HAYDEN, founder of Resilient New Media Inc.

"Stephanie Forbes masterfully connects history to modern execution, capturing my attention from Romans and sharks through to managing global events and chaos. This book cuts through theory and offers practical insight for leaders and practitioners working across complex global value chains."

—BRIAN LANIER, president of The Leaders Circle and former regional vice president of Starbucks

"*Global Wealth, Local Impact* speaks to the realities of work today: complexity, constraint, and constant change. Stephanie Forbes offers an accessible, experience-based framework for understanding how value chains create outcomes, not just movement. Her focus on strategy, governance, negotiation, partnerships, risk, and performance measurement makes this a valuable resource for both emerging professionals and seasoned practitioners. We have trusted Stephanie to help us develop high-quality programs that stand up in the real world, and this book reflects the same discipline, experience, and clarity. I highly recommend it."

> —**TIM OGILVIE,** vice president and dean of MCG Career College and chair of the Alberta Association of Career Colleges, Canada

"Wow! Once I picked this book up, I couldn't put it back down. A practical guide to supply-chain leadership and management, from strategy to tactics, *Global Wealth, Local Impact* considers a broad range of disciplines across the network. I found this book insightful, informative, and so very timely given the ever-growing complexity of today's value chain. Using both historical examples and todays modern-day realities & challenges, this book is an excellent guide as we look towards optimizing a truly global supply chain network."

> —**DAVID KINDER,** president and CEO of Big Rock Brewery

"Global Wealth Local Impact is a timely and practical guide for supply chain professionals charged with the accountability for navigating the complex world of global sourcing and operations. Resiliency, visibility, and risk management are key to successful twenty-first century supply chain management, and Stephanie Forbes brings the theory of the concepts to life with practical applications."

> —**PATRICK ETOKUDO,** managing partner at ANKANVCM

"Stephanie Forbes brings clarity and heart to one of the most complex topics in modern business. This is a masterclass in how to add extraordinary value while creating iron-clad risk management in today's turbulent supply chain ecosystem."

—**LAURIE KENLEY,** founder of Silica Intelligence

"This book proves how the secret to a business' success lies in its ability to work magic in its supply chain management. Stephanie cleverly gets to the underbelly of what makes or breaks an organization through its ability to manage its value chain. A highly entertaining read steeped in history and practicality, Stephanie illustrates that while we may encounter never before circumstances with changes in geo-politics and tech advancements, success leaves clues. We can and should lean on lessons from the most successful organizations in history."

—**CATHERINE LAM,** CPA, CMA, managing partner and COO of Blue Sky Consulting

"There are books that inform, and then there are books that reposition how you see the world. *Global Wealth, Local Impact* is the latter. Stephanie Forbes doesn't write from theory or trend. She writes from the trenches, from lived experience, earned wisdom, and a deep respect for the people who quietly hold the global economy together.

"This book honors the unseen architects of value while challenging leaders to think bigger, act braver, and lead more responsibly.

"What I love most about Stephanie is her clarity. She doesn't romanticize complexity, she translates it. She doesn't chase noise, she delivers substance. Page after page, she connects strategy to humanity, global systems to local consequence, and leadership to accountability in a way that feels both grounded and visionary.

"This is not a book you skim. It's a book you sit with. A book that sharpens your thinking and expands your leadership lens. A book that reminds us that real impact isn't accidental, it's intentional.

"Stephanie Forbes has given us more than a framework. She's given us a call to lead with intelligence, integrity, and impact, at scale.

"If you care about leadership that lasts, systems that matter, and decisions that ripple far beyond the boardroom, this book belongs on your desk, and in your hands."

—**SCHARRELL JACKSON,** international keynote speaker, global executive coach, author, and founder and CEO of Leadership in Heels

"This book is a powerful reminder that supply chains are not just operational systems, they are strategic levers that shape businesses, economies, and communities. Stephanie Forbes brings clarity, depth, and real-world wisdom to a complex topic every modern leader must understand."

—**AJ VADEN,** CEO and cofounder of Brand Builders Group and *New York Times* bestselling author of *Wealthy and Well-Known*

GLOBAL WEALTH
LOCAL IMPACT

HOW SUPPLY CHAINS BUILD THRIVING COMPANIES, CULTURES, AND COUNTRIES

STEPHANIE FORBES

MDP | MISSION DRIVEN PRESS

Published by Mission Driven Press, an imprint of Forefront Books, Nashville, Tennessee.
Distributed by Simon & Schuster.

Library of Congress Control Number: 2026902916

Print ISBN: 978-1-63763-516-2
E-book ISBN: 978-1-63763-517-9

Cover Design by George Stevens, G Sharp Design LLC
Interior Design by Bill Kersey, KerseyGraphics

Printed in the United States of America

26 27 28 29 30 31 RR4 10 9 8 7 6 5 4 3 2 1

DEDICATION

To the professionals in the trenches—to the ones who keep the world moving.

This book is dedicated to you:

the project buyers,
the contract specialists,
the category managers,
the warehouse supervisors,
the schedulers,
the planners,
the customs brokers and freight forwarders,
the supply chain analysts,
the logistics coordinators,
the quality inspectors,
the operations leads,
the ERP admins,
the chief procurement officers,
the inventory managers,
the major projects teams.

To every professional who is pulling double shifts, mapping routes through chaos, chasing better terms, turning uncertainty into strategy, and solving problems in real time.

To those working in fast-moving consumer goods, manufacturing, oil and gas, health care, transportation, aerospace, defense, tech, retail, construction, agriculture, and every other corner where value chains are built and rebuilt daily.

Whether you manage multibillion-dollar capital projects or track containers across the ocean, this book is for you.

You are the ones who show up early, stay late, and solve problems no one else wants to touch or sees coming.

You balance cost, risk, schedule, and quality—often with limited resources and little fanfare.

This is your playbook.

CONTENTS

FOREWORD

BY DYLAN BARTLETT

The global business environment has never been more complex, volatile, or interconnected. In the past few years, we have seen unprecedented supply chain disruptions—from pandemics to geopolitical tensions and environmental crises. These events have peeled back the curtain on a system that, for decades, operated quietly in the background. Suddenly, executives, consumers, and governments are acutely aware of how critically dependent our modern world is on the intricate and often fragile network of global supply chains.

This new reality has created a pressing need for a fresh perspective on supply chain management, one that moves beyond static theory and into the dynamic, real-world strategies required for resilience and success. This is precisely the need that Stephanie Forbes addresses with clarity and insight in this book.

I have had the privilege of knowing Stephanie for a number of years, working closely together on many supply chain initiatives. Her expertise in this field has always been distinguished by both a rare ability to anticipate change and a solutions-oriented approach to risk mitigation. I have seen firsthand how Stephanie navigates complexity and provides actionable, forward-thinking guidance to leaders who are facing seemingly impossible challenges.

In this book, Stephanie Forbes distills a career's worth of experience and insight into a powerful, accessible framework. Instead of offering a dry academic text, she provides a road map for understanding and mastering the modern supply chain. You will find compelling case studies on supply chain resilience, practical steps for integrating new technologies, and strategies for ethical sourcing. Stephanie doesn't just explain concepts—she illuminates how to put them into practice.

For the experienced supply chain professional, this book offers a crucial reevaluation of best practices and an introduction to the next generation of strategies. For the executive who needs to understand the strategic importance of their supply chain, it demystifies a critical aspect of modern business and shows how it can be a source of competitive advantage. For the student, it provides an end-to-end perspective that connects theory to the real-world demands of the market.

This is not just another book on logistics. It is an essential guide for anyone who seeks to not only survive but thrive in the face of ongoing disruption. Stephanie Forbes has given us more than a book; she has provided a compass for the turbulent waters ahead. Read it, and you will not only understand why your supply chain is important—you will also know how to make it your most powerful asset. And remember:

The future of the supply chain belongs not to those who can predict every storm but to those who build a system strong enough to weather any.

Dylan Bartlett
President and CEO, Supply Chain Canada

WHEN GETTING THERE IS HALF THE BATTLE—AND KEEPING THINGS ALIVE IS THE OTHER HALF

You're a Roman *claviger* (dock worker) in 46 BCE, and your boss, aka Magister Navis, just dropped the mother of all procurement requests in your lap: "Caesar needs three live sharks for next week's gladiator games. Oh, and we need to make sure they're hungry."

Just another Tuesday in ancient Rome's supply chain nightmare.

Before you start updating your LinkedIn profile to "Roman Shark Guy," consider the sheer magnificence of this logistical feat. We're talking about transporting multiple apex predators across the Mediterranean, keeping them alive, and ensuring they maintain that perfect balance between "hungry enough to be entertaining" and "not so hungry they start to float upside down." And you thought your last-mile delivery issues were bad.

But here's the kicker: The Romans actually pulled this off. They developed sophisticated systems to transport live fish and other marine creatures across vast distances, using specialized vessels with built-in water tanks. Sometimes the sharks arrived dead or the Romans swapped them out for dolphins—close enough, right?—but the mere attempt speaks volumes about their supply chain capabilities.

This, dear reader, is where our journey into the fascinating world of *value chains* begins. From Roman shark procurement to modern-day semiconductor shortages, from Silk Road caravans crossing deserts to automated warehouses shipping across continents with a click, from the East India Company's trading fleet to SpaceX's dreams of interplanetary supply chains, the fundamental challenges remain surprisingly similar: How do we get stuff from point A to point B without losing our shirts—or, in ancient Rome's case, our sharks?

History offers many fascinating approaches to supply chain management. Let's take a quick look at three:

1. Rome's logistical precision

2. The Silk Road's collaborative networks

3. The East India Company's corporate dominance

Each tackled the challenge of moving goods across vast distances with distinctly different styles.

First, the Romans built an empire on standardization and infrastructure. Their 250,000 miles of roads connected three continents, with way stations every twenty miles and a logistics system that could move everything from grain to live sharks—yes, really—across the Mediterranean.[1]

Their approach: If you can't move goods easily, build a road—and protect it with an army.

Second, the Silk Road stretched over four thousand miles, connecting Chang'an to Constantinople through a web of independent traders. At its height during the Tang Dynasty (618–907 CE), it moved not only precious silk—worth its weight in gold in Rome—but also ideas, technologies, and cultural innovations across continents.[2]

Their approach: Create standards and let commerce flow naturally.

Third, the East India Company took things in a more corporate direction. By 1800, they'd grown from a simple trading venture to controlling territory with 20 percent of the world's population, commanding a 250,000-strong private army, and generating revenue equivalent to $4.9 trillion in today's terms.[3]

Their approach: vertical integration, shared risk, and market intelligence.

Each system left lasting legacies that shape modern supply chain thinking: Rome's genius for standardization and infrastructure—every road the same width, every mile marked, every port designed to common specifications; the Silk Road's master class in collaborative networks and cultural intelligence—where trust and relationships mattered more than contracts; and the East India Company's innovations in corporate structure and risk management—they invented modern marine insurance and stock markets, after all.

The lesson for modern supply chain managers? Build robust infrastructure like the Romans, nurture relationships like the Silk

Road traders, and manage risk like the East India Company—but remember that sustainable success comes from creating value at each step in the value chain, not just controlling it. After all, two of these empires fell, while the Silk Road's principles of mutual benefit and adaptable networks still shape global trade today.

BEYOND MOVING BOXES: UNDERSTANDING VALUE CHAINS

The Evolution of Value Creation

What turned Rome from a collection of seven hills into an empire that spanned continents? It wasn't only their legions—it was their mastery of value chains. The Romans understood something fundamental: Success isn't just about moving stuff around; it's about creating value at every step.

Consider their road network:

- They didn't just build paths; they created highways of commerce

- They didn't just connect cities; they connected economies

- They didn't just transport goods; they transported ideas

- They didn't just move armies; they moved civilization itself

Sound familiar? Today's value chains do exactly the same thing, just with fewer togas and more technology.

From Supply Chains to Value Chains: The Critical Difference

A *supply chain* gets things from here to there. A *value chain* transforms them along the way. Think of it this way:

Supply Chains	Value Chains
Move products	Create possibilities
Focus on efficiency	Focus on effectiveness
Connect points	Connect purposes

Let's be clear—a value chain is not just a fancy term for "how stuff gets places." If it were, we'd still be using the Roman method of sending a guy to run really fast with important messages until he dropped dead. Fun fact: That's where the marathon comes from, and it's possibly the worst delivery Key Performance Indicator (KPI) in history.

A Global Value Chain (GVC) is the entire process through which a product or service gains value at each step, from conception to delivery. A GVC includes the following stages:

- Ideation

- Design and Development

- Manufacture and Production

- Contracting

- Projects

- Marketing

- Distribution

- Transportation and Logistics

- Waste

- Post-Sale Support

- Disposal (including the recycle-and-reuse circular economy)

These activities are spread across multiple countries, each region contributing people, raw materials, manufacturing, services, technology, transport, and so on. GVCs are shaped by geopolitical, economic, technical, social, environmental, legal, and regulatory factors, and each stage adds value to the overall process and impacts how benefits are distributed globally.

Consider our Roman shark example:

- Someone had to source the sharks

- Someone else had to figure out how to transport them

- Another person had to keep them alive

- Yet another poor soul had to make sure they were properly "hangry" for the show

- And finally, someone had to convince the gladiators that it was a great career opportunity

Each step added value, albeit in a way that would give modern OSHA representatives heart palpitations.

WHY THIS MATTERS TODAY

You might be thinking, *That's fascinating, but I work in tech/manufacturing/retail, and we definitely don't deal with hangry sharks.* (Unless you're reading this at SeaWorld, in which case, carry on.)

But here's the thing: Today's supply chains are just as complex, if not more so. Instead of figuring out how to transport live sharks across the Mediterranean, you're trying to source semiconductors during a global shortage. Instead of keeping marine preda-tors alive in wooden vessels, you're maintaining temperature-controlled supply chains for COVID-19 vaccines. Instead of feeding sharks just enough to keep them interested in gladiatorial combat, you're managing inventory levels to keep your customers interested without drowning in holding costs.

The tools have changed (thank goodness for Excel), but the core challenges remain:

- Getting stuff where it needs to be

- Keeping it in the condition it needs to be in

- Doing it all without bankrupting the empire—or your company

- Managing risks, from pirate attacks to cybersecurity breaches

- And most importantly, adding value at every step

As we delve into the intricacies of modern value chains, we'll traverse a landscape that spans tactical dilemmas—like avoiding a shortage—and forging strategic partnerships—far less fatal than the alliances that brought sharks to Roman amphitheaters. We'll uncover negotiation tactics sharper than a Silk Road trader's wit and explore ways to navigate inflation without resorting to minting coins with less silver than integrity (a nod to the fiscal experiments of later Roman Caesars).

But before we get too deep, let's take a moment to marvel at how far humanity has come. No matter the scale of today's supply chain headaches, at least you're not tasked with drafting a procurement order that reads: "Three live sharks, must arrive hungry, delivery just in time 3:00 p.m. Tuesday."

Welcome to the ever-evolving world of value chains. Buckle up—it's going to be an unforgettable journey.

THE JOURNEY AHEAD: YOUR GUIDE TO VALUE CHAIN MASTERY

This book is your road map through the complexity of modern value chains. Think of it as your personal guide to not merely surviving but thriving in the wild world of global commerce.

We'll take you from the Roman Empire, along the Silk Road, and across the high seas of the East India Company, highlighting how their innovation and strategies revolutionized how we move goods and services around the world today.

Resources have been developed to provide additional information and organizational tools, which are available online. Visit globalwealthlocalimpact.com/resources for immediate gratification.

What You'll Learn Along the Way

We'll trace the evolution of value chains from ancient Rome's amphitheater logistics to the AI-powered fulfillment engines of today. Along the way, you'll uncover timeless principles, modern best practices—without the bloated consulting fee—and future-proof strategies that help your business outlast economic curveballs, regulatory demands, and, yes, trends that fade faster than powdered British wigs. Each chapter is grounded in real-world examples, actionable frameworks, and a little wit, covering everything from daily operations to boardroom negotiations, and from metrics that matter to partnerships that don't implode under pressure.

Let's begin with the foundational elements of supply chains that have stood the test of time.

Seven Critical Aspects of Value Chain Management

As we work through this book together, you'll learn how to master the seven critical aspects of value chain management and be able to implement them in your workplace.

The critical aspects are represented in each of the following chapters. We'll talk about the different theories, where they occurred in history, and how they can be applied now to demonstrate the timelessness of the concepts.

Those aspects are:

1. Tactical Excellence:
   Because someone still needs to make sure the widgets arrive on time.

2. Strategic Vision:
   Because crystal balls and coin flips aren't a strategy.

3. Negotiation Mastery:
   Because "win-win" beats "win-lose"—especially when sharks are involved.

4. Partnership Building:
   Because no supply chain is an island.

5. Economic Navigation:
   Steering through a financial storm without losing cargo.

6. Measurement Systems:
   Because you can't improve what you can't measure—and can't explain to the board.

7. Global Event Response:
   Because stuff happens, and it's usually not in the plan.

The world of value chains is changing faster than a Roman chariot with a nitro boost. But some things remain constant: the need to get the right stuff to the right place at the right time, the importance of building strong relationships, and the eternal truth that somewhere, somehow, something in your supply chain is probably going wrong right now.

But that's okay. Because by the time you finish this book, you'll have the tools, insights, and, I hope, a sense of humor about it all.

CHAPTER 1

THE GREAT TRADE ROUTES

Rome was the original logistics powerhouse. Before there were global supply chains, there was Rome—a city that ran on logistics long before the term was coined. At its height, the Roman Empire was a marvel of centralized planning, engineering innovation, and sheer logistical ambition. Spanning three continents and over five million square kilometers, the empire wasn't just held together by legions of soldiers; it was powered by an intricate supply network designed to move grain, wine, olive oil, and building materials across vast distances.[1]

Take the example of Rome's food supply. The city, with more than a million inhabitants at its peak, required approximately 200,000 tons of grain per year, much of it sourced from Egypt and North Africa.[2] This wasn't simply a matter of convenience; it was survival. Without reliable supply chains, a city as densely populated as Rome would have faced constant famine.

Enter the Roman port of Ostia, a logistics hub that could rival any modern-day container terminal. Cargo ships unloaded grain into warehouses, called *horrea*, where it was stored, measured, and distributed using an early version of inventory management systems. And this was all done without spreadsheets or ERP (Enterprise Resource Planning) software.

Rome's supply chain wasn't only about feeding the populace; it was designed to fuel the empire's ambition. Grand construction projects like aqueducts, amphitheaters, and roads required colossal amounts of material—stone, timber, metals, and the infamous lead pipes. These materials had to be sourced, moved across vast distances, and assembled with surgical precision. Take the Pantheon, for instance. Its domed roof, still standing today, used self-healing Roman concrete. Craftsmen embedded lime clasts, or lime fragments, in the concrete, which reacted with water over time to reseal cracks—an innovation we're only now beginning to replicate.[3]

What made all this possible wasn't just Roman engineering; it was the supply chain. Rome had the ability to move virtually anything: people, animals, lead, timber, lime. Their system of sourcing and distributing materials was the backbone of their empire and a foundational prototype of today's value chains.

The Appian Way, one of Rome's most strategic roads, served both military and commercial purposes. It moved troops, yes, but also trade goods, ideas, and culture. To streamline this trade across provinces, the Romans introduced standardized weights and measures, ensuring a jug of olive oil sold in Gaul matched one sold in Alexandria. In short, they weren't just building infrastructure; they were building the infrastructure of trust.

Innovation was at the heart of Roman logistics. They built a fleet of merchant ships with flat bottoms to navigate shallow waters, ensuring year-round trade even in challenging conditions.

They developed the *cursus publicus*, a state-run courier and transportation system that moved goods and messages faster than any camel caravan on the Silk Road. Think of it as the Roman Empire's version of FedEx—complete with roadside inns, called *mansiones*, for drivers and relay stations for fresh horses.

But not all Roman supply chain innovations were sustainable. The empire's insatiable demand for exotic goods—silk from China, spices from India, and ivory from Africa—led to severe trade imbalances, much like today's global trade concerns. Roman coins flowed out of the empire in exchange for luxury goods, but that money did not return, as the Romans did not make any goods worth the same amount as precious silk and spices. This depleted their reserves of silver and gold.

By the time later emperors figured out that the constant outflow of silver and gold was always a debit and never a credit, they resorted to debasing the currency, reducing the precious metal content of coins with inferior metals. Meanwhile, the empire was already grappling with significant inflation and economic instability, which undermined its foundations.[4]

The lessons from Rome are as relevant now as they were two thousand years ago.

ROME'S LESSONS

Centralized Planning

Rome thrived on its ability to coordinate resources across vast distances, a principle modern supply chains still rely on.

Infrastructure Investment

The empire's roads, ports, and aqueducts were the backbone of its logistics system, proving that infrastructure is the foundation of any successful supply chain.

Standardization

Whether it was weights, measures, or the design of *amphorae* (tall jars for storing olive oil or wine), the Romans understood the efficiency of standardization—a concept still central to supply chain optimization.

Overreach Risks

Rome's eventual decline reminds us that even the most advanced supply chains can falter when stretched too far, too fast, or without adapting to changing circumstances.

Rome wasn't just an empire of soldiers and senators; it was an empire of supply chain managers, logistics planners, and infrastructure innovators. From feeding a million people to building some of the most iconic structures in history, Rome's legacy is a testament to the power of supply chains to create—and *sustain*—civilization.

THE SILK ROAD: THE ORIGINAL GLOBAL NETWORK

Long before we had the internet, we had the Silk Road—the world's first information superhighway with actual highways. Picture a trade network spanning four thousand miles, connecting cultures that couldn't speak one another's languages, using currencies that weren't always compatible, and somehow managing to move both goods and ideas across the most challenging terrain on earth. If that sounds familiar to modern supply chain managers, it should.

The Silk Road wasn't only about silk—though Roman merchants paid their weight in gold for those shimmering fabrics. It was the world's first truly integrated supply chain network, complete with rest stops called *caravanserais*, quality control—counterfeit silk was apparently a thing even then—and complex financing arrangements, the original letters of credit.

Consider the story of Zhang Qian, the Han Dynasty explorer who essentially became the world's first market researcher. Sent west to gather intelligence about potential markets, he returned thirteen years later with something far more valuable than silk: information. He mapped out potential trading partners, identified market demands, and even conducted what we'd now call competitive analysis of rival trade routes.[5] Modern supply chain managers spend millions on market research to achieve what Zhang did with an assistant, a few camels, and a lot of patience.

The Silk Road's success relied on five fundamental principles that still resonate today:

1. **Cultural Intelligence**
   The merchants were obviously good at buying and selling, but they were masters at understanding local customs and preferences. They learned quickly that selling silk to nomads required different tactics than selling to Roman aristocrats. Today's global supply chain managers face similar challenges, though with fewer camels and more Zoom calls.

2. **Information Flow**
   The Silk Road's true innovation wasn't in moving goods; it was in moving information. Merchants shared details about market prices, route conditions, and political changes. A

price change in Chang'an, modern Xi'an, could influence trading decisions in Rome months before the goods arrived. This is something many of us are familiar with today: News from Asian manufacturers still affects Western markets.

3. Network Effects

The Silk Road was a network of interconnected routes, each adding value to the whole. Each new connection did more than add another point on the map; it created exponential possibilities for trade. Modern supply chain managers call this *network optimization*, but the principle remains the same: The strength of a network lies in the number of connections, not simply its overall size.

4. Innovation Adaptation

The most famous example of Silk Road industrial espionage—smuggling silkworm eggs in hollow walking sticks—demonstrates how innovation spreads through supply chains. Those smuggled silkworms eventually created new production centers, changing the entire trade dynamic.[6] Today, we call this *technology transfer* and write lengthy legal contracts about it, but the principle remains: Innovations rarely stay contained.

5. Resilience

Perhaps the most relevant lesson from the Silk Road is about resilience. When one route became blocked—by weather, politics, or bandits—traders found alternatives. They built redundancy into their networks, maintained multiple supplier relationships, and always had contingency plans. In an era where a single blocked canal can disrupt global trade, we could learn something from those ancient traders who never put all their silk in one caravan.

The Silk Road's ultimate legacy demonstrates the power of organic trade networks and cultural exchange. At its height during the Tang Dynasty (618–907 CE), this network of trade routes stretched over four thousand miles, connecting Chang'an to Constantinople, with branches extending to Korea, Japan, Southeast Asia, and Eastern Africa. The scale was staggering: Caravans could include up to a thousand camels, each carrying as much as five hundred pounds of goods, representing millions in today's currency per journey.[7]

The network's significance went far beyond silk, though the fabric commanded extraordinary prices in Rome—one pound of silk sold for about 600 grams of gold.[8] The routes carried everything from paper and gunpowder from China to glass and olive oil from Rome, to spices and precious stones from India. More crucially, they transmitted ideas, technologies, and cultural practices: Buddhism spread from India to China, papermaking moved westward, and artistic styles blended across cultures.

The Silk Road's decline came gradually through multiple factors rather than a sudden collapse. The fall of the Mongol Empire in the fourteenth century reduced the political unity that had made long-distance trade safer. The rise of maritime trade routes offered cheaper, faster alternatives for bulk goods. The devastating Black Death from 1346 to 1353, which likely spread along these very trade routes, disrupted commerce and population centers. By the time the Ottoman Empire captured Constantinople in 1453, cutting off the western end of the traditional overland routes, the Silk Road's golden age had already passed.[9]

The Silk Road's influence endures in modern global commerce. It established patterns of international trade, demonstrated the importance of standardized exchange practices—caravanserais were the first standardized rest stops, complete with banking services—and showed how decentralized networks can be resilient. Today's supply chain managers recognize these same principles: the power of standardization, the importance of relationship networks, and the value of diverse routing options.

The Silk Road proved that successful supply chains don't always need central control—sometimes they need well-established protocols and mutual interest.

THE EAST INDIA COMPANY: CORPORATE EMPIRE BUILDING 101

If the Silk Road was the world's first global network, the East India Company was the world's first multinational corporation on steroids. Imagine Amazon, Walmart, and the US Navy combined, complete with its own army and the ability to mint currency. That was vertical integration on a historic scale.

The Company, as it was simply known, wasn't content with merely moving goods around; it created an entire ecosystem of trade that would impress and slightly intimidate modern supply chain managers. At its height, it controlled half the world's trade and had a private army twice the size of Britain's.

Talk about taking supply chain security to the extreme.

Author and historian William Dalrymple notes that the East India Company started as a small enterprise with just over a hundred shareholders and a royal charter, yet it ultimately expanded into a force that governed much of the Indian subcontinent. And while corporate armies are no longer on the table—the HR paperwork alone would be nightmarish—the Company's vertically integrated supply chain management still offers some fascinating lessons.[10]

The Company's innovations in supply chain management centered on four key principles that still resonate:

1. Vertical Integration

The Company controlled more than just the shipping. It also owned the ports, warehouses, production facilities, and even the markets where goods were sold. When faced with piracy, they didn't file insurance claims; they built a navy. Having supply chain problems? Simply acquire the entire country producing your goods. While modern businesses can't quite take it to that extreme, the principle of controlling critical parts of the supply chain remains relevant.

2. Financial Innovation

They pioneered complex financial instruments like shares, bonds, and insurance products to fund and protect their operations. The Company effectively created the modern stock market, insurance industry, and corporate finance—all to solve supply chain problems. Today's supply chain financing may be more sophisticated, but the fundamental challenges of funding global operations remain similar.

3. Market Intelligence

The Company maintained an extensive network of agents and informants who provided real-time—as real-time as sailing ships allowed—information about market conditions, political developments, and trading opportunities. These "factors" were essentially the world's first global market research team, complete with competitive intelligence gathering that would impress modern corporate espionage units.

4. Risk Management

Operating in distant markets with long lead times forced the Company to develop sophisticated risk management strategies. They diversified their cargo, developed insurance schemes, and maintained buffer stocks in stra-tegic locations. When storms sank ships or markets crashed, they had systems in place to absorb the shock—a lesson modern supply chain managers are relearning in the age of global disruptions.

The Company's ultimate lesson is about the dangers of unchecked power in supply chain control. They transformed from a trading company into what was effectively a sovereign power, controlling everything from production to distribution, from governance to monetary policy.

Their downfall came from corruption, mismanagement, and overextension. The Company's monopolistic practices led to devastating consequences, including the Bengal Famine of 1770, which killed an estimated one-third of Bengal's population.[11] Their aggressive expansion resulted in costly wars, while financial mismanagement and widespread corruption among Company officials created instability. The final blow came with the Indian Rebellion of 1857, which forced the British government to nation-alize the Company and take direct control of India.

By 1874, the Company that had once ruled an empire was formally dissolved. The British Parliament's intervention, including the East India Company Act of 1773 and the Charter Act of 1833, marked the world's first major corporate regula-tions, setting precedents for government oversight of private enterprise. Modern supply chain managers might note that while vertical integration can bring efficiency, building collab-orative networks rather than monopolistic control tends to be more sustainable and ethical.

The East India Company's legacy lives on in modern supply chain management—minus the colonial infrastructure. Their innovations in corporate finance, insurance and risk management, and market intelligence established foundational business practices we still use today: the modern stock market, corporate reporting structures, and risk mitigation tools, like insurance.

MODERN CHALLENGES, ANCIENT WISDOM

Did our Roman friend ever stop to verify that the shark delivery actually contained sharks? Or did they end up with dolphins instead? After all, both have fins, teeth, and hail from the Mediterranean. Close enough—right?

It's a reminder that some supply chain problems are timeless: confusing documentation, fuzzy product specs, and a delivery that technically meets the criteria . . . but doesn't quite deliver. The tools have changed—from scrolls to spreadsheets—but the headaches remain remarkably familiar.

The more things change, the more they stay the same.

Let's dive into the original four pillars of governance—principles that have kept value chains upright since the days when an unlucky Roman legionnaire received the ancient equivalent of a high-priority Slack ping:

> ·URGENT—From Caesar's desk: Need three (3) live sharks for next week's games. Must be XL size. Teeth intact. NO SUBSTITUTIONS.

Now imagine trying to enforce that procurement spec. What was the Roman version of a service-level agreement when your inventory was actively trying to eat your logistics team? Who was forced to confirm that the teeth were indeed "intact"? And was there some poor soul measuring each shark to verify compliance with Caesar's XL-size expectations?

This wasn't just spectacle; it was early governance in action: specifications, verification, risk, and a whole lot of plausible deniability. And if that shark turned out to be a dolphin?

Well, welcome to ancient supply chain fraud.

These weren't merely one-off challenges. The Romans ran an "exotic animals for entertainment" supply chain that makes Amazon's logistics look like a kids' lemonade stand. We're talking about sourcing, transporting, and housing roughly one million animals over the Colosseum's active period—from lions and tigers and bears (oh my!) to elephants, giraffes, and, yes, our finicky friends the sharks. Add to that the logistics of managing roughly half a million gladiators and prisoners—talk about complicated human resources!—and you've got yourself a supply chain nightmare that makes even the most seasoned modern logistics manager wake up in a cold sweat.

To put this in perspective: Imagine running a modern zoo, a military operation, and a professional sports league simultaneously, where your inventory was trying to eat your employees, your athletes were often reluctant participants, and your CEO had a habit of feeding underperformers to the lions when deliverables were late. And you thought your performance reviews were tough!

The four pillars of governance keep a value chain grounded when complexity, chaos, or even Caesar's latest request threatens to throw everything off course. From fraud prevention to financial oversight, these timeless principles form the backbone of operational integrity. Let's take a closer look at how they've held up—from ancient amphitheaters to modern boardrooms.

Pillar #1: Fraud Prevention—Trust but Verify

Fraud has been an ever-present challenge throughout the history of trade, from ancient Rome to the modern supply chain. In an era when trust was often the only currency, merchants and governments alike developed sophisticated systems to protect the integrity of their goods and transactions. One of the earliest examples came from ancient Rome, where *amphorae* containing olive oil or wine were sealed with stamped clay markers. These stamps identified the producer, ensured the contents remained authentic, and signaled the quality of the product.

While simple, this system acted as a deterrent to fraud, as breaking or altering the seal was punishable under Roman law. Merchants caught tampering with goods faced severe penalties, ranging from fines to public shaming, exile, or "signing" up for the introductory gladiator training program at the Colosseum.

On the Silk Road, fraud prevention assumed new complexities. Counterfeit silk was a significant issue, as unscrupulous traders tried to pass off lower-quality fabrics as the real thing. *Caravanserais* served as roadside inns and rest stops where traders rested and exchanged goods, playing a critical role in verifying the authenticity of products. These hubs relied on trusted local inspectors or senior merchants who could authenticate goods, ensuring buyers avoided being swindled.

The East India Company in the seventeenth and eighteenth centuries also faced fraud on a global scale, as counterfeit spices and low-quality textiles could easily undermine trust in their brand. To combat this, the Company implemented a system of quality control audits at their warehouses in key locations such as Calcutta, Madras, and London. Goods that did not meet their stringent standards faced outright rejection. This attention to quality solidified the Company's reputation and helped them dominate global markets.

Modern parallels to these practices include the widespread use of blockchain technology in supply chains. Blockchain provides an unalterable digital ledger that records every step of a product's journey, from source to destination, ensuring authenticity and traceability. This is particularly important in industries like luxury goods, pharmaceuticals, and food safety. Fraud prevention remains a constant in supply chains, evolving from stamped clay and *caravanserai* inspections to QR codes and digital tracking.

Key takeaways:

Verification Systems: From Roman *amphorae* stamps to Silk Road inspections, authentication mechanisms build trust and deter fraud.

Quality Assurance: Rigorous standards, like those employed by the East India Company, ensure customer confidence and brand integrity.

Modern Innovations: Blockchain and digital technologies provide new ways to combat fraud in global, complex supply chains.

Trust is the foundation of trade, but verification is what keeps it standing.

Pillar #2: Financial Management—Follow the Money

Financial management is the lifeblood of any trade network, ensuring resources flow seamlessly to sustain operations. Ancient Rome showcased an advanced understanding of financial systems through its *aerarium*, the state treasury. Revenue from taxes, tributes, and trade allowed the Romans to fund massive public works, including aqueducts, roads, and the construction of the Colosseum.

Roman tax collectors operated a complex system to track transactions across the empire, ensuring resources flowed in and out efficiently. For example, records from Ostia, Rome's primary port, reveal meticulous bookkeeping practices that accounted for every shipment of grain arriving from Egypt.

The Silk Road introduced new levels of financial innovation to facilitate long-distance trade. Letters of credit, precursors to modern financial instruments, enabled merchants to trade goods without carrying large sums of money—an essential safeguard against banditry. These documents served as guarantees of payment, honored by trusted financiers along the trade route.

A notable example of this occurred during the Tang Dynasty (618–907 CE), when traders in Chang'an could use credit notes to secure goods in Samarkand or Constantinople, reducing the risk of theft and streamlining commerce.

The East India Company revolutionized financial management on a global scale. By the eighteenth century, the Company pioneered joint-stock ownership, allowing investors to pool resources and share risks. This innovation laid the groundwork for modern corporate finance and made the Company a financial powerhouse. They also introduced marine insurance as a safeguard for their shipping fleets, ensuring that even if a ship carrying valuable goods sank en route to London, the financial impact was minimized. Additionally, their extensive use of bills of exchange enabled capital to flow seamlessly between their hubs in London, Bombay, and Canton, facilitating large-scale trade without the physical transfer of gold or silver.

Modern supply chains have built on these historical innovations with technologies like real-time payment tracking, automated reconciliation systems, and financial analytics tools. Yet the fundamental questions remain the same: How do we ensure funds are available where needed, transactions are secure, and costs are managed effectively?

The practices of the Romans, Silk Road traders, and the East India Company remind us that sound financial management is essential for the sustainability of any value chain.

Key takeaways:

- **Efficient Resource Allocation:** From Rome's *aerarium* to the Silk Road's letters of credit to East India's bills of exchange, liquidity and transparency have always been essential.

- **Financial Risks:** Innovations like marine insurance and cargo load distribution demonstrate the value of financial safeguards.

- **Scalability:** Joint-stock ownership, pioneered by the East India Company, enabled trade networks to grow without overextending capital.

Financial management across history teaches us that while the tools evolve, the principles of securing and managing resources remain unchanged.

Pillar #3: Oversight—Even Romans Needed Traffic Laws

Governance is the backbone of any trade system, ensuring consistency and order. The Romans excelled at this through their highly organized legal and logistical systems.

Roman law provided clear rules for contracts, property rights, and trade disputes, fostering trust across the empire. For example, their *Lex Claudia* regulated the amount of *amphorae* (300) a single boat could carry, and it was designed to limit foreign influence in Roman matters by encouraging local, land-based development.

Infrastructure governance was equally meticulous: The Appian Way featured standard widths, mile markers, regular maintenance schedules, and rules of the road, which enabled the efficient movement of goods and people across the empire.

On the Silk Road, governance took a more decentralized form but was no less effective. *Caravanserais*, scattered along the routes, served as hubs of regulation and standardization. Merchants relied on these rest stops for currency exchange and weight calibration. Local administrators also served as arbiters for conflict resolution and enforced trade agreements, ensuring smooth operations despite the lack of centralized control.

The East India Company brought corporate governance to new heights. Their governance system included charters and codes of conduct for employees, as well as a board of directors in London overseeing operations from India to China. However, their failure to adequately address corruption and monopolistic practices led to disastrous consequences and forced the British government to impose stricter regulations, such as the Regulating Act of 1773.

Today's governance frameworks, including ISO certifications and compliance regulations, echo these historical practices. Clear rules, standardized procedures, and effective oversight remain critical for ensuring that global trade networks function smoothly and ethically. As history shows, the cost of neglecting governance can be catastrophic.

Key takeaways:

Legal Frameworks: Roman commercial law and East India charters demonstrate the importance of clear rules for trade.

Standardization: From Roman road markers to Silk Road *caravanserai* scales, consistency fosters trust and efficiency.

Corporate Accountability: The downfall of the East India Company illustrates the dangers of unregulated power and the need for oversight.

Consistent oversight is the invisible hand that guides commerce, ensuring that even the most complex systems function with order and integrity.

Pillar #4: Risk Management—Expecting the Unexpected

Effective risk management has been a hallmark of successful supply chains throughout history, and few organizations mastered it better than the East India Company. Operating from the early seventeenth century to its dissolution in 1874, the Company faced a staggering array of risks: storms at sea, piracy, geopolitical upheavals, and market fluctuations. Their ability to anticipate, adapt, and mitigate these challenges was central to their dominance in global trade for centuries.

One of the East India Company's greatest innovations was the development of marine insurance, which became a cornerstone of risk management in the shipping industry. By the late 1600s, the Company was insuring its ships and cargo through the burgeoning insurance market at Lloyd's Coffee House in London, the precursor to Lloyd's of London.[12]

This practice ensured that losses from shipwrecks, storms, or pirate attacks did not bankrupt the Company. For example, when the *Grosvenor*, an East India ship carrying valuable cargo, sank off the coast of South Africa in 1782, the insurance payouts allowed the Company to recover financially and continue its operations without interruption.[13]

The Company also implemented redundancy and diversification as risk mitigation strategies. Ships rarely traveled alone;

instead, they sailed in convoys to deter pirates and spread the risk of loss.

Additionally, the Company maintained multiple trade routes and alternative ports to ensure that blockades or political disruptions never fully stopped their operations. For instance, when hostilities with France escalated during the late eighteenth century, the Company shifted its operations to avoid contested waters and ensure a steady flow of goods from India and China to Britain.

In their supply chain management, the East India Company also maintained strategic reserves of goods. Warehouses in London, Calcutta (modern-day Kolkata), and Canton (modern-day Guangzhou) stocked tea, spices, textiles, and other high-demand items, creating reserves that buffered against market volatility and supply disruptions. When the Company faced a shortage of Chinese tea due to restrictions imposed by the Qing Dynasty in the 1750s, these stockpiles allowed it to continue meeting demand in Europe without significant price increases.[14]

The Company's approach to risk management extended to geopolitical strategy. They often secured exclusive trading rights and formed alliances with local rulers, such as the Mughal Empire in India, to ensure the stability of their operations. However, these strategies were not without their challenges. The Great Bengal Famine of 1770, exacerbated by the Company's monopolistic practices, revealed the dangers of overcentralized control and poor contingency planning during agricultural failures and population crises.

In addition to managing physical and financial risks, the East India Company excelled at information-based risk mitigation. Their network of "factors," or agents, and informants provided "real-time" intelligence on market conditions, political developments, and potential threats. This intelligence allowed the Company to make informed decisions and adapt quickly to changing circumstances. For example, during the Opium Wars of the mid-nineteenth century, this intelligence network helped the Company navigate the volatile trade environment in China.[15]

The lessons from the East India Company's risk management practices resonate strongly today. Whether safeguarding ships laden with goods in the eighteenth century or mitigating cyber-attacks on digital supply chains in the twenty-first century, as always, the fundamentals remain the same. Risk management is about anticipating threats, building resilience through redundancy, and leveraging information to adapt to ever-changing conditions.

Key takeaways:

Insurance as a Buffer: Early marine insurance mitigated financial losses from inevitable risks like storms and piracy.

Redundancy in Networks: Convoys, alternative trade routes, and stockpiled goods ensured continuity in the face of disruptions.

Strategic Alliances: Partnerships with local rulers and governments reduced geopolitical risks and opened new markets.

Intelligence Networks: Continuous information flow provided the agility to adapt to rapidly changing conditions.

By the time the Company was dissolved in 1874, its legacy had transformed risk management into a science. Modern supply chains continue to draw inspiration from these principles, demonstrating that effective risk management is timeless. Whether navigating eighteenth-century oceans or twenty-first-century digital networks, the ability to expect the unexpected is the key to resilience.

THE MODERN VALUE CHAIN LANDSCAPE

Today's supply chain managers may not deal with live predators—unless you count office politics—but they navigate challenges that make ancient logistics look quaint. Let's explore the storm of complexities facing modern value chains—and why it's both a nightmare and a fascinating puzzle.

Technological Disruption: When the Future Arrives Before You're Ready

If you'd told a Roman centurion that one day we'd have metal birds carrying cargo across oceans, he'd probably offer you a cup of watered-down wine and suggest you sleep it off. And yet, here we are—living in a world where robots organize warehouses, blockchain tracks avocados, and AI predicts inventory demand better than your most seasoned analyst.[16]

The technological revolution isn't only about better tools; it's also about rewriting the rules. AI is the new soothsayer, providing predictive analytics that make the Oracle at Delphi look amateurish. Automation has turned warehouses into symphonies of robotic efficiency, where forklifts are conductor-less and everything hums in unison—until one machine decides it's time for a "software nap."

Consider the Internet of Things (IoT). With sensors on everything from pallets to produce, your inventory now texts you updates. Need to know where your lettuce is? Check your phone. Blockchain, meanwhile, ensures that every link in the supply chain is transparent, making fraud obsolete, much like clay seals on *amphorae*.

Even digital twins—virtual replicas of supply chains—are becoming standard. Imagine a Roman official trying to model weather disruptions with a clay tablet. Now compare that to a digital twin simulating a typhoon's impact on port operations in real time. It's like trading in a chariot for a hyperloop.

But let's not sugarcoat it: Technology doesn't come without headaches. Implementation is costly, systems require constant updates, and—let's be honest—convincing your team to embrace automation can still feel like herding cats. Still, there's no turning back. Technology is no longer the future; it's the present, and it's moving faster than we can update our apps.

Environmental Pressures: Because Having a Planet Is Important

Modern supply chain managers wake up at 3:00 a.m. wondering how to balance carbon footprints, recycling mandates, and net-zero goals. Environmental considerations have gone from fringe concerns to boardroom priorities, and they're not going anywhere.

Take carbon footprints. Companies are now under pressure to calculate, track, and reduce their emissions—often across sprawling global operations. Circular economies are the new frontier, with businesses finding creative ways to recycle, repurpose, and reduce waste. It's no longer enough to ship a product; you also need a plan for what happens when it's returned, reused, or—ideally—never wasted in the first place.

And let's talk about climate change. Floods, droughts, and hurricanes are catastrophic for supply chains. In 2024, the US experienced twenty-seven separate climate-related events. Each resulted in over $1 billion in damage. In fact, between 1980 and 2024, the US experienced a whopping 403 climate disaster events, each causing $1 billion of damage.[17] These events are global. The EU experienced drastic climate events in 2024 as well. Flooding throughout the EU contributed to 335 deaths with damages reaching €18 billion just that year. The impacts are as unpredictable as they are expensive.[18]

The real challenge? Balancing sustainability with profitability. How do you go green without going broke? It's a logistical Rubik's Cube, made more difficult by the rapid pace of regulatory change. Companies that crack the code, however, find that sustainable practices often lead to long-term cost savings and stronger customer loyalty.

Global Complexity:
When "It's Complicated" Becomes a Business Strategy

The Romans thought managing a lone empire was tough. I'd like to see Caesar try to navigate today's labyrinth of global trade. Between shifting geopolitical alliances, ever-changing trade regulations, and the sheer pace of cultural and technological shifts, the global landscape makes the Roman Empire look like a well-organized backyard barbecue, and trade regulations change more frequently than Roman emperors in the year 69 CE (that's a history joke for the nerds like me—there were four of them).[19]

Let's start with geopolitical tensions. Pirates may have been the bane of the East India Company, but today's supply chains face trade wars, tariffs, and sanctions that can upend entire industries overnight. A single social media post can disrupt markets faster than any barbarian raid. Just ask the companies caught off guard by Brexit or the US-China trade dispute.

Then there are trade regulations. Modern compliance requirements make Roman bureaucracy seem downright charming. Tariffs appear and disappear like a magician's coin trick, while documentation demands grow more labyrinthine by the day. Supply chain managers must be part diplomat, part legal expert, and part fortune teller to navigate the chaos.

Add to that the challenge of cultural considerations. A campaign that does great in Tokyo might flop in Texas, and a negotiation style that works in Paris might confuse suppliers in Mumbai. Understanding local nuances is no longer optional; it's essential.

There's also market volatility. From the pandemic-induced chaos of 2020 to the infamous *Ever Given* container ship blocking the Suez Canal, disruptions can come from anywhere.[20] One day your supply chain is humming along; the next, you're scrambling to explain delays to a very impatient board.

The Triple Threat

Modern value chains face a trifecta of challenges:

1. **Technology** evolving faster than adoption can keep up

2. **Environmental pressures** demanding immediate action

3. **Global complexity** adding layers of unpredictability

But here's the silver lining: With challenges come opportunities. Companies that embrace innovation, invest in resilience, and adapt to change will continue to prosper in the future. Tools like predictive analytics, sustainability frameworks, and advanced automation transform value chains into strategic assets.

Innovation Hurdle: We Can No Longer Say, "We've Always Done It This Way"

The Romans revolutionized transportation with their roads—networks that connected their empire, facilitated trade, and stood the test of time. Modern value chains redefine what's possible. Instead of simply connecting places, they connect people, technology, and ideas across a far more complex world.

New Business Models, Disruption is the New Normal

Trade may be as old as civilization itself, but the business models driving modern value chains are anything but traditional. Disruption has become the standard operating mode, and today's supply chains evolve faster than anyone imagined even a decade ago. What were once straightforward systems of buying, storing, and delivering goods have morphed into ecosystems designed for speed, efficiency, and adaptability.

Take, for example, the rise of "Supply Chain as a Service" platforms. These networks allow businesses to rent logistics capabilities—everything from warehouse space to transportation fleets—rather than owning them outright. It's the supply chain equivalent of Uber: Why own it when you can rent it?

Similarly, virtual inventories upend traditional warehousing. Instead of centralizing goods in physical storage facilities, businesses now use predictive analytics and decentralized systems to track inventory as it moves. Products essentially exist "everywhere and nowhere," allowing companies to fulfill orders more quickly and efficiently.

Then there exist crowd-sourced delivery networks, which have redefined the last mile of logistics. By leveraging independent contractors—think gig economy couriers—companies can meet consumer demands for faster delivery without the overhead of managing fleets.

Meanwhile, micro-fulfillment centers, located closer to urban populations, ensure same-day or even same-hour delivery becomes possible.

New business models thrive on turning inefficiencies into opportunities, proving that the greatest disruptions often come from reimagining the rules of the game.

Emerging Technologies, From the Impossible to the Everyday

Roman aqueducts were cutting-edge engineering, comparable to today's emerging technologies that seem like nothing short of Star Trek–style science fiction brought to life. The tools shaping modern value chains rewrite the very nature of logistics, manufacturing, and consumer engagement. For example:

Autonomous Vehicles: Self-driving trucks and drones no longer represent distant dreams; they now deliver goods faster and with fewer emissions. These "metal chariots" reduce costs and reshape transportation logistics.

Quantum Computing: This revolutionary technology has the potential to solve problems that currently seem unthinkable. Imagine optimizing global shipping routes, factoring in weather, traffic, and fuel efficiency across millions of variables—in seconds. It's the next frontier of efficiency.

3D Printing Networks: Why ship a product when you can print it on demand? Distributed manufacturing transforms industries like health care and automotive, reducing lead times and cutting transportation costs.

Beyond these headline-grabbing technologies, AI-driven predictive analytics and the Internet of Things (IoT) create supply chains that think and communicate. Sensors on everything from pallets to perishable goods give real-time updates, ensuring nothing is lost or wasted. Meanwhile, blockchain creates trust networks that render fraud as obsolete as broken clay seals on amphorae on the Silk Road.

If the Romans relied on clay tablets and human labor to manage logistics, we now have digital twins—virtual replicas of entire supply chains that simulate disruptions and optimize performance. It's not merely progress; it's a paradigm shift.

Market Expansion, A Marketplace Without Borders

While the Romans expanded markets through conquest, today's businesses expand through connectivity. The boundaries that once defined markets have been erased by technology, creating opportunities that are global, digital, and deeply personal.

Consider the rise of digital marketplaces like Amazon and Alibaba. These platforms connect millions of buyers and sellers, operating as 24/7 commerce hubs that span the globe. Then there's virtual reality shopping, where consumers explore immersive digital stores, try on products virtually, and make purchases with a swipe or click.

Modern businesses also leverage personalization at scale. Using advanced analytics, companies tailor products and services to individual preferences, creating stronger consumer loyalty and engagement. Meanwhile, direct-to-consumer (D2C) models eliminate middlemen, allowing brands to build deeper relationships with their customers while improving margins.

The result? Markets are no longer limited by geography or traditional distribution models. They're defined by innovation, consumer expectations, and the ability to adapt. The Romans may have built an empire one province at a time, but modern companies build global empires with the click of a button.

Sustainability Leadership, Building a Future Worth Living In

The Romans built roads and aqueducts to last for centuries, but modern value chains aim for something even greater: sustainability. Today's thought leaders rethink how value chains impact the planet, societies, and economies, turning sustainability from a buzzword into a business imperative. Consider:

Circular Supply Chains: These systems recycle and repurpose resources, ensuring that waste becomes input for new production. Think of it as the ultimate upgrade to the Roman approach of reusing construction materials.

Zero-Waste Initiatives: Companies find innovative ways to eliminate waste, from converting food scraps into biofuels to repurposing industrial by-products.

Renewable Energy Integration: Solar and wind power become standard in production facilities, reducing reliance on the grid and fossil fuels while cutting emissions.

Biodegradable Packaging: Unlike the scrolls lost to fire in ancient Rome, modern packaging is designed to disappear—on purpose.

Sustainability also extends to social and economic dimensions. Fair labor practices, ethical sourcing, and community impact programs now remain central to value chains. Companies realize that long-term success depends on creating value not only for shareholders but for all stakeholders.

THE BOTTOM LINE: YESTERDAY'S ROADS STILL LEAD FORWARD

If Roman roads were built to last, modern value chains must be built to adapt. The pace of change in today's world—from global pandemics to climate change and technological disruption—requires systems that remain resilient, flexible, and scalable. This includes:

Flexible Networks: Supply chains now function like living organisms, able to reroute and reconfigure in response to disruptions.

Adaptive Technologies: AI and automation enable real-time decision-making, so companies respond promptly to shifts in demand or supply.

Resilient Partnerships: Strong alliances with suppliers, customers, and even competitors help ensure stability in uncertain times.

Scalable Solutions: As demand grows, so, too, must the systems that support it—without sacrificing efficiency or increasing costs.

Modern value chains are much more than just pipelines for goods—they're ecosystems for innovation, collaboration, and resilience.

The winners in this new landscape are those who innovate fearlessly, sustain responsibly, adapt quickly, and create value that endures. Modern challenges may be greater, but so are the possibilities.

CHAPTER 2

TACTICAL MASTERY

Sarah Chen's phone buzzed at exactly 6:00 a.m., signaling the start of another unpredictable day. Her automated warehouse management system in Phoenix had detected an anomaly in the picking patterns and reorganized the fast-moving SKUs for better efficiency. Normally, this would be a win, but today it felt more like a curveball. A major promotion was starting in just three hours, and the picking team hadn't been briefed on the new layout. Efficiency collided with chaos before the sun even rose.

Fifteen minutes later, an email arrived from Taiwan, where her largest supplier had experienced a power outage that halted production for at least twelve hours. On paper, her safety stock levels showed she should be covered, but Sarah had learned to trust her instincts as much as her spreadsheets—and her instincts were whispering, "This could get messy."

By 6:30 a.m., chaos escalated. A Slack message from Marketing dropped into her notifications with a casual bombshell: "We're launching a flash sale! Just a small promo—25 percent off our top one hundred items!" The same top one hundred items that her warehouse AI had just reorganized.

The timing was impeccable, as usual. Sarah sighed, knowing these kinds of surprises were simply part of the job.

Supply chain management in the modern world isn't for the faint of heart. Every day is a high-stakes puzzle where the pieces keep changing shape, and Sarah had become an expert at keeping up. The Romans might have had to worry about feeding live sharks during transport, but at least they didn't have to coordinate with Marketing.

THE TACTICAL TOOLBOX: THEN AND NOW

By 8:00 a.m., Sarah was monitoring two eerily similar situations unfolding on her dual monitors. On the left, her Phoenix facility was handling a sudden 300 percent spike in orders for air purifiers—a direct result of nearby wildfires turning the air quality hazardous. On the right, her Dallas warehouse faced an almost identical surge in demand for the same products, this time due to a surprise dust storm sweeping through the region.

The two facilities may have been managing the same product and the same spike in demand, but that's where the similarities ended.

Phoenix, equipped with the latest in supply chain technology, was practically self-governing. AI algorithms had automatically adjusted picking routes, reorganized inventory positions, and coordinated with nearby facilities to share the load. The system had even sent capacity alerts to suppliers and rerouted orders to optimize delivery timelines. It was like watching a self-conducting orchestra, every note perfectly in tune.

Dallas was a different story. Running on legacy systems due for an upgrade next quarter, the warehouse team was struggling to keep up. Picking paths had to be adjusted manually, phone calls flew between departments, and the backlog grew by the minute. Team leaders worked heroically to manage workflows, but without real-time data or automation, they were playing a frantic game of catch-up.

By the end of the day, the outcomes were stark. Phoenix had fulfilled 98 percent of its orders, maintained standard delivery times, and even managed to optimize shipping costs despite the surge. Dallas, despite the team's best efforts, achieved only 73 percent fulfillment, with overtime costs piling up and delivery delays frustrating customers.

Sarah knew the difference wasn't in the dedication of the teams or the physical capabilities of the facilities. It was in the tools they had at their disposal—and, more importantly, how those tools were being implemented.

The disparity reminded Sarah of something she often said in team meetings: "Tools are only as good as their implementation." Without strategic planning, even the most advanced technology becomes little more than expensive clutter.

The lessons of the past were clear. The Romans, for all their innovation, had the same basic infrastructure across their empire, yet some provinces prospered while others struggled. The difference wasn't in the roads or aqueducts but in how local leaders leveraged these tools to meet their needs.[1]

Sarah thought about her Phoenix and Dallas facilities in this light. Phoenix had mastered its digital arsenal, creating a seamless ecosystem where every tool was integrated and every decision was data-driven. Dallas, on the other hand, resembled a Roman outpost still relying on manual labor and outdated maps.

The tools weren't the problem.

What was holding them back was a lack of integration and strategy.

BUILDING THE DIGITAL ADAPTATION FRAMEWORK

Sarah knew building an effective tactical toolbox required more than simply buying the latest technology. It required a structured approach to implementation, something she thought of as the **Digital Adaptation Framework**.

At the base of her framework lay **Foundation Systems**. This included the fundamental infrastructure: data collection tools, standardized operating procedures, and comprehensive training for teams. Without this, even the most advanced AI system would crumble under the weight of unorganized data.

The next component, **Integration**, connected systems to create a real-time data flow. It emphasized cross-functional coordination and the use of analytics to turn raw data into actionable insights.

Next were **Intelligence Systems**, where AI and machine learning came into play. These systems not only analyzed data; they predicted disruptions and automated decision-making, leaving humans free to focus on strategy.

The **Adaptation Mechanisms** followed, enabling systems to self-adjust based on changing conditions. From learning algorithms to dynamic resource allocation, this level transformed static systems into agile networks.

Finally, the **Innovation Platform**—a space for continuous improvement and cultural transformation. This was where companies integrated new technologies, evolved their processes, and fostered a mindset of constant growth.

Sarah knew the path to success wasn't about adopting technology for technology's sake. It was about creating a system that could adapt, evolve, and succeed in the face of constant change. Whether managing the daily grind of warehouse alerts or planning for long-term growth, the key was strategy—and the willingness to learn from both the past and the present.

Although Sarah is a fictional character, the truth remains that any transformation requires a foundation be put in place first. Depending on your organizational goals and needs, once the foundation is established, the other four parts of the framework can develop concurrently or sequentially. Keep in mind, they will develop at different rates.

Digital Adaptation Framework

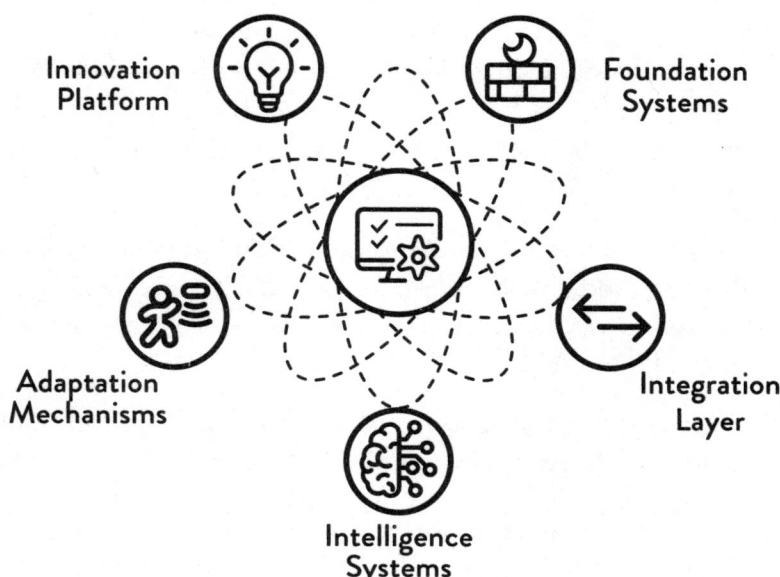

The future of supply chain technology is vast and often under-resourced. The future will bring more technology we already know, like digital twins, blockchain verification, and quantum computing applications.[2] However, we've learned that all the technology in the world won't help if your team keeps using "password123" to log in. Looking at you, Dave from IT.

OPERATIONS MUST-HAVES

There are four concepts that must be continually monitored when it comes to delivering in a tactical environment. They're time, resources, quality, and crisis management.

Time Management:
Because Time Waits for No Supply Chain

In the fast-paced world of supply chain management, time isn't just money; it's survival. Modern supply chains must juggle multiple overlapping timelines to keep goods moving efficiently. Lead times, the duration between ordering and receiving inventory, are critical for managing production schedules and customer expectations. A single delay in lead time can cascade into missed delivery windows and unhappy customers.

Processing times, or the speed at which goods are prepared for shipping, add another layer of complexity. Facilities must balance speed with accuracy, ensuring that orders are fulfilled promptly without sacrificing quality.

Transit times, the duration it takes for goods to travel from point A to point B, pose additional challenges, especially with the rise of same-day and next-day delivery services.

Finally, there's the intangible factor of customer patience, which, in today's on-demand economy, seems to hover around

3.7 seconds.[3] Meeting these expectations requires meticulous coordination, robust tracking systems, and a culture that prioritizes efficiency. In this world, every minute matters, and supply chain managers live by the mantra: *Deliver faster, deliver smarter, and never keep a customer waiting.*

Modern Tactics Requiring Balancing

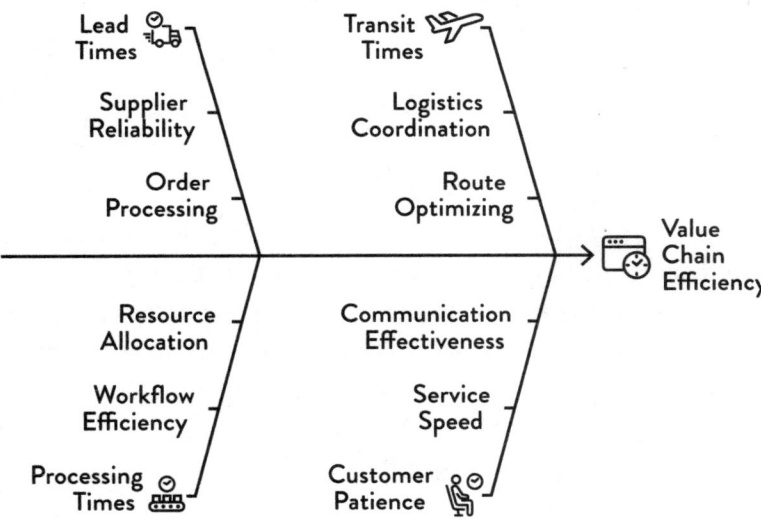

Resource Allocation: Playing Tetris with People, Machines, and Money

Resource allocation in supply chains is like playing a never-ending game of Tetris, except the blocks are people, machines, and budgets—and they're all flying at you fast and furious—and sometimes sideways or upside down.

Labor scheduling is a critical piece of the puzzle. Humans need breaks, training, and predictable schedules, while robots operate tirelessly until they require maintenance or recharging. Balancing these two types of labor is a science in itself, ensuring that neither humans nor machines become underutilized or overworked.[4]

Equipment utilization is another key consideration. Expensive machinery, such as automated sorting systems or forklift fleets, must remain operational to justify their cost. Downtime is the enemy, and supply chain managers constantly analyze usage patterns to keep equipment running smoothly.

Space optimization is yet another challenge, as warehouses play a game of Jenga, optimizing boxes, pallets, and inventory flows. Every square foot counts, and poor space management can lead to bottlenecks that slow down the entire operation.[5]

All this happens under the constraints of a budget that never seems to stretch far enough. Managers must make tough decisions about where to invest—whether in labor, technology, or infra-structure—while still meeting financial targets. Effective resource allocation is more than simply balancing the books; it also requires ensuring that every person, machine, and dollar contributes to the overall efficiency and success of the supply chain.

Quality Control: Because "Good Enough" Never Is

In a world where customers expect perfection, quality control is nonnegotiable. Modern supply chains have evolved far beyond manual inspection lines, leveraging cutting-edge technology to ensure that every product meets or exceeds standards.

Automated inspection systems, powered by AI and machine vision, identify defects in milliseconds, catching issues that are impossible for the human eye to detect. Real-time quality moni-toring further enhances this process, providing continuous feed-back that enables immediate corrections.

Optimizing Resource Allocation in Supply Chains

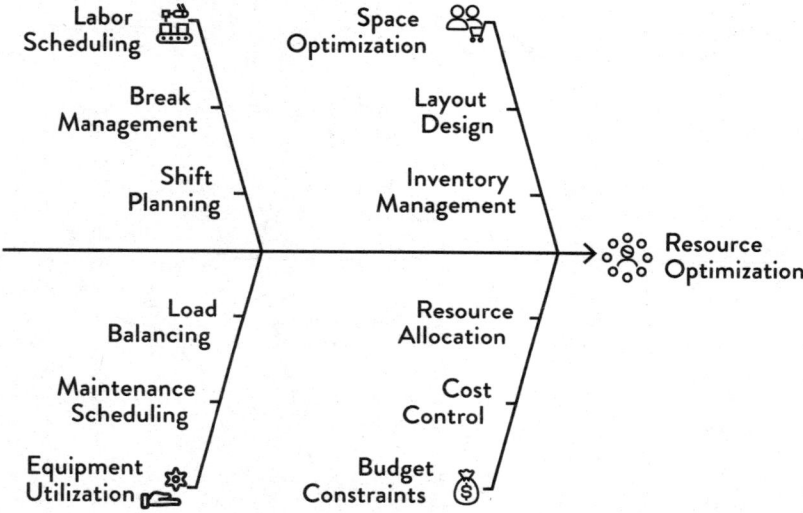

Predictive maintenance plays a crucial role in maintaining quality. By analyzing data from sensors on production equipment, supply chain managers can predict when a machine is likely to fail and address the issue before it disrupts operations.[6]

Error-proofing processes, such as *poka-yoke*—a Japanese technique designed to prevent human errors—are also standard practice.[7] These systems ensure that mistakes get caught and corrected before they reach the customer, preserving both brand reputation and customer trust. In modern supply chains, "good enough" is *never* good enough. Excellence is the only acceptable standard.

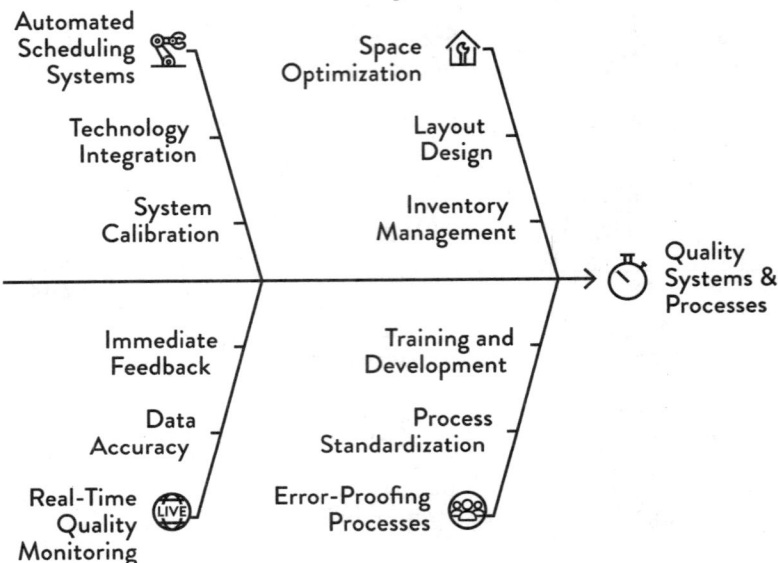

Modern Quality Control Tactics

Crisis Management: Because Something Always Goes Wrong

No matter how well-oiled the machine may be, something inevitably goes wrong. Whether it's a natural disaster, a supplier failure, or a sudden surge in demand, crises are an unavoidable reality of supply chain management.

The key to surviving—and thriving—in these moments is preparation. Contingency planning is the first line of defense, involving detailed strategies for managing potential disruptions. From alternative suppliers to rerouted transportation networks, these plans ensure the supply chain adapts quickly to changing circumstances.[8]

Real-time problem-solving is another essential skill. When a crisis hits, supply chain managers must act swiftly, using live data to make informed decisions. Escalation procedures are equally critical, providing a clear chain of command and communication protocols to prevent confusion during high-pressure situations. Customer communication rounds out the tactical response, as transparency can make or break a company's reputation during a crisis. Clear, honest updates reassure customers that their needs remain prioritized, even in the face of adversity.

Crisis management isn't merely about reacting to problems— it's about building a resilient supply chain capable of withstanding disruption. As the saying goes: *Hope for the best but prepare for the worst*. In supply chain management, that preparation makes all the difference.

Tactical Responses to Crisis Management

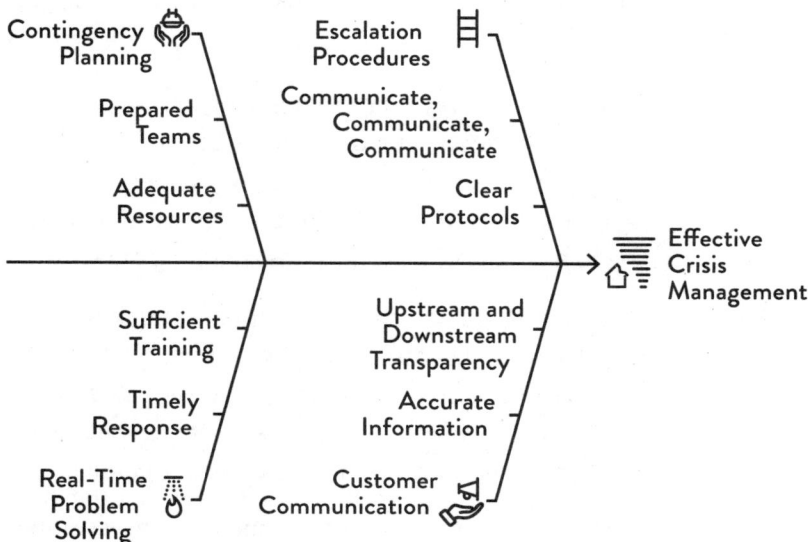

TACTICAL SUCCESS METRICS

Supply chain management thrives on data. Without clear metrics, even the most advanced systems risk wandering into inefficiency. Tactical success begins with establishing the right KPIs to evaluate performance, identify weaknesses, and drive continuous improvement. Crucial KPIs for most supply chains include:

Order Accuracy: Ensuring the right product reaches the right place at the right time isn't only about meeting expectations—it's also about avoiding costly mistakes. A single error can trigger returns, lost sales, and customer dissatisfaction, making this KPI nonnegotiable for any operation.

Inventory Turnover: Keeping inventory moving is critical for profitability and to avoid obsolescence. High turnover rates signal an efficient supply chain, while low rates can lead to clogged warehouses and wasted capital. The goal is to strike a delicate balance between availability and excess.

On-Time Delivery: In today's on-demand economy, on-time delivery is the cornerstone of customer satisfaction. Late shipments don't merely frustrate customers; they erode trust and loyalty. Meeting delivery promises requires precision across the entire supply chain, from procurement to last-mile logistics.

Cost per Order: Financial efficiency matters as much as operational efficiency. Cost per order tracks how much it takes to process, pack, and deliver each unit. Keeping these costs under control without sacrificing service quality is a constant balancing act, ensuring fiscal accountability and future business viability.

Metrics like these transform abstract goals into measurable results, providing the insights necessary to refine systems, allocate resources, and build resilience.

Putting It All Together: The Modern Tactical Playbook

Mastering supply chain tactics means building systems that adapt, evolve, and endure. The modern tactical playbook distills years of lessons into five actionable principles that any supply chain professional can apply:

1. **Start with Good Data**

   The adage "garbage in, garbage out" applies to every system, from AI-driven forecasting to inventory management.[9] Clean, accurate data is the foundation of every successful operation. Invest in tools and processes that ensure data integrity and consistency.

2. **Use Technology Wisely**

   Technology can transform operations, but blind reliance is a recipe for disaster. Automation and AI should complement human decision-making, not replace it. Trust the systems, but verify their outputs.

3. **Build Flexible Systems**

   Disruptions are inevitable, whether they come from a natural disaster, a cyberattack, or a robot staging a workplace rebellion. Flexible systems with built-in redundancies and contingency plans are essential for surviving the unexpected.

4. **Keep the Human Element in Mind**

   Supply chains depend on people—customers, employees, and suppliers. Respecting their needs and perspectives is both good ethics and good business. Engaged employees, communicate transparently with customers, and build trust with suppliers.

5. Plan for Failure

Optimism is not a strategy. Even the best-laid plans can fail, and the key to resilience is being ready when they do. Develop and regularly test contingency plans for critical processes to ensure your supply chain can recover quickly and effectively.

These principles form the backbone of modern supply chain management, balancing innovation with practicality and technology with humanity.

THE BOTTOM LINE: DISCIPLINE AND ADAPTATION

Tactical mastery in modern supply chain management is less about following a static playbook and more about orchestrating a dynamic, ever-changing performance. Picture a conductor managing an orchestra where half the musicians are robots, the other half are humans distracted by their phones, and the audience still expects perfection every time. It's a challenge, and—on good days—an incredibly rewarding endeavor.

The Romans managed to transport live sharks across the Mediterranean without GPS, smartphones, or robot warehouses. They succeeded because they focused on the fundamentals: meticulous planning, robust systems, and a willingness to adapt when things went wrong—ergo, some dolphins in the mix. While today's tools are vastly more sophisticated, the core principles remain the same: Get the right product to the right place at the right time, preferably without losing your sanity in the process.

So, the next time you're tempted to curse at an overzealous warehouse robot or lament a delayed shipment, take a moment to be thankful. At least you're not captaining an East India Company ship, braving pirate-infested waters and unpredictable monsoons, all while negotiating with distant rulers for trade rights.[10]

Modern supply chains may feel chaotic, but unlike the merchants of old, we have the tools to turn complexity into opportunity—no treasure maps or cannons required. Then again, explaining to a customer that their package is late because a robot reorganized the warehouse? That might be an even tougher challenge.

CHAPTER 3

STRATEGIC VISION

Picture a Silk Road merchant planning their route from China to Rome. Along with the basic logistics of which route to take, he had other questions to answer. Which kingdoms might rise or fall? Which new trade routes might emerge or be blocked by war? Which competitors might undercut his prices—or engage in industrial espionage? For centuries, Damascus steel was the envy of every empire—swords that could cut through armor yet bend without breaking. The formula was a fiercely guarded secret. When the Crusaders brought samples back to Europe, metallurgists spent decades trying to replicate its pattern and strength, marking one of the earliest known cases of reverse engineering.[1]

Fast-forward a few millennia, and today's supply chain teams face similarly complex strategic challenges. Strategic vision goes far beyond *predicting* trends; it's about actively *shaping* them. When Elon Musk built his Gigafactory in Nevada, he was addressing an immediate need: creating the products that will move the world toward more sustainable energy consumption.

He was also, however, reimagining the entire electric vehicle supply chain.[2]

That's the essence of strategic vision: anticipating where the play is going now, while also anticipating where the entire game might be played in the future.

For supply chain professionals, strategic vision is the difference between playing checkers and chess. Successful players visualize the entire board, anticipate their opponent's moves, and build a strategy three steps ahead. Whether navigating geopolitical risks, integrating new technologies, or positioning your network to seize new opportunities, the goal is clear: Design a system that's resilient, adaptable, and always a step ahead of disruption.

BUILDING YOUR EMPIRE

Great supply chains, like great empires, don't emerge by accident—they're built. Strategic network design is the cornerstone of this empire-building process. Much like Roman generals planned the roads and garrisons to maintain control over distant provinces, modern supply chain professionals must design networks that balance efficiency, resilience, and opportunity.[3]

Network Design: Because Location, Location, Location

In the days of the Silk Road, network design was as much an art as a science. Merchants chose their routes based on a mix of geography, alliances, and market demand. Today, network design has evolved into a highly sophisticated process, but the principles remain the same. It's about positioning your operations in the right places, reaching the right markets, and balancing costs against risks.

Critical considerations include:

Geographic Positioning

Where you locate your warehouses, factories, and distribution centers can make or break your supply chain. In the Roman Empire, this meant building granaries near fertile regions and ports near trade hubs. Today, it's about proximity to raw materials, customer bases, and transportation infrastructure. For example, companies like Amazon strategically position fulfillment centers near major population centers to enable same-day delivery.[4]

Market Access

A well-designed network connects your products to the right customers at the right time. This might mean opening facilities in high-growth markets like Southeast Asia or establishing local partnerships to navigate complex regulatory environments. The East India Company excelled at this, building trading posts across Asia and India to access local goods while maintaining direct lines to European markets.[5]

Risk Distribution

The phrase "don't put all your eggs in one basket" also applies to supply chain strategy. Companies that relied heavily on single regions—like East Asia for manufacturing—faced major disruptions during COVID-19. Modern network design prioritizes diversification: Multiple suppliers, geographically dispersed facilities, and contingency plans for rerouting production or shipments in the event of disruptions.[6]

Cost Optimization

Balancing cost efficiency with resilience is the eternal struggle of network design. Cheap labor or materials might draw a company to one region, but hidden costs like tariffs, shipping delays, or environmental risks can eat into profits. Strategic thinkers use tools like digital twins to simulate cost scenarios and identify the optimal mix of price and performance across global networks.[7]

WHAT SHAPES THE FUTURE OF SUPPLY CHAINS?

Once the network is designed, the next step is developing strategic initiatives that keep the supply chain competitive, resilient, and aligned with long-term goals. Three critical areas demand attention: technology integration, competitive positioning, and risk management. Let's break these down a bit.

Technology Integration: From Abacus to AI

Supply chain management has always been shaped by technology, from the invention of the abacus to the rise of modern AI. Each breakthrough has expanded the possibilities and transformed how businesses operate, compete, and innovate. Today, technology integration is no longer optional. It has become the foundation of strategic supply chain management. However, simply adopting technology isn't enough. Success depends on how well these tools are chosen, implemented, and aligned with long-term goals.

Digital Transformation Road Maps

Digital transformation is a journey, not a one-off project. Organizations need a clear road map to ensure their technology investments deliver value. This road map begins with an honest assessment of current capabilities and gaps. Where are inefficiencies dragging down performance? Which processes are ripe for automation or improvement? Once these questions have answers, businesses can prioritize investments, focusing on initiatives that drive the most significant impact.

A successful digital transformation road map includes measurable milestones, cross-functional collaboration, and a commitment to adaptability. For instance, Maersk, the global shipping giant, embarked on a digital overhaul that prioritized transparency and customer engagement. By implementing real-time tracking and predictive analytics, they transformed the shipping experience, providing clients with visibility from port to port.[8]

Platform Selection and Integration

Choosing the right platforms is critical for any technology strategy. The market is flooded with tools promising to optimize everything from inventory management to last-mile delivery, but not all platforms are created equal. Strategic leaders focus on selecting solutions that align with their operational goals and integrate seamlessly with existing systems.

Integration is where many technology projects stumble. A new platform may offer impressive features, but if it operates in isolation, it adds complexity rather than simplifying operations. Imagine a warehouse management system that doesn't communicate with transportation software—inventory might be perfectly managed, but delivery schedules could still fall apart. The key is interoperability. Companies like Procter & Gamble have excelled by adopting end-to-end platforms that unify data across procurement, manufacturing, and distribution, enabling a cohesive and agile supply chain.[9]

Automation Strategy

Automation is often the most visible aspect of supply chain technology, from robotic pickers in warehouses to self-driving trucks on highways. But automation goes beyond replacing manual tasks with machines. It's also about redefining workflows to maximize efficiency and flexibility.

Take Amazon, whose Kiva robots revolutionized fulfillment centers by bringing shelves to workers instead of the other way around. This innovation didn't just speed up operations; it allowed Amazon to redesign warehouse layouts entirely, increasing storage density and throughput.[10] Automation strategies must be tailored to the organization's needs, balancing cost with long-term value and ensuring that human workers are empowered rather than displaced.

Data Analytics Capabilities

In supply chain management, data is power. Companies that harness analytics gain a competitive edge, transforming raw information into actionable insights. Predictive analytics, for example, can forecast demand surges, identify bottlenecks, and recommend proactive solutions. Meanwhile, real-time dashboards provide visibility across the supply chain, allowing managers to make informed decisions in moments.

One standout example is Walmart, which uses advanced analytics to optimize inventory and anticipate customer behavior. By analyzing purchasing trends and local events, the retail giant ensures shelves are stocked with the right products at the right time. The result? Reduced waste, increased sales, and happier customers.[11]

But with great data comes great responsibility. Companies must invest in data governance, ensuring accuracy, security, and compliance. Without these safeguards, even the most sophisticated analytics systems can lead to flawed decisions or expose the organization to regulatory risks.

From the Silk Road's use of tally sticks to track trade transactions to today's AI-driven supply chains, technology has always been a force multiplier for commerce. But modern supply chain professionals know that technology is only as effective as the strategy behind it. It's not about adopting the latest buzzwords; it's about selecting the right tools, implementing them with precision, and using them to drive measurable outcomes.

The organizations that master technology integration will lead their industries toward the future. After all, while the tools have evolved from abacus to AI, the goal remains the same: Build a supply chain that is efficient, resilient, and future-ready.

COMPETITIVE POSITIONING— ZAGGING WHILE EVERYONE ELSE ZIGS

In the high-stakes world of supply chain management, you have no choice but to stand out.

Competitive positioning is the art and science of creating a distinct edge that sets your supply chain apart from the rest. Much like chess players anticipate opponents' moves, businesses must anticipate market shifts, customer demands, and competitor strategies to stay ahead. Sometimes, this means finding opportunities in overlooked areas or crafting innovative solutions that redefine the game.

Market Differentiation

Market differentiation is the cornerstone of competitive positioning. It's about answering a critical question: What makes your supply chain better, faster, or smarter than the competition? The answer lies in creating unique value for customers, whether through cost leadership, superior service, or cutting-edge technology.

Take Zara, the Spanish fashion giant, as a prime example. Zara built its empire on the back of an agile supply chain that differentiates itself through speed and responsiveness. While competitors take months to bring new designs to market, Zara's vertically integrated supply chain allows it to go from concept to store in just three weeks. This rapid turnaround keeps customers coming back, creating a competitive edge that others struggle to replicate.[12]

Core Competency Development

To truly stand out, companies must invest in developing their core competencies—the unique capabilities that drive their competitive advantage. These competencies are often built around operational strengths, such as logistics efficiency, product innovation, or customer experience.

Amazon's core competency lies in its unmatched logistics network. From its vast network of fulfillment centers to its last-mile delivery capabilities, Amazon has created a supply chain so efficient that it can offer same-day delivery for millions of products. This logistics prowess is the foundation of Amazon's market dominance and a key reason why competitors struggle to keep up.[13]

Competitive Advantage Creation

Competitive advantage isn't simply about being good at what you do; it's about being irreplaceable. This often involves leveraging unique resources, proprietary technology, or exclusive relationships to create value that others can't easily replicate.

Consider Apple, whose supply chain is a master class in competitive advantage. From securing exclusive agreements with suppliers for cutting-edge components to designing custom logistics solutions, Apple's supply chain is a tightly controlled ecosystem that supports its premium pricing and market leadership. By aligning its supply chain strategy with its broader business goals, Apple has created a system where every component, process, and partnership reinforces its competitive position.[14]

Strategic Partnerships

In today's interconnected world, no company can succeed alone. Strategic partnerships are a powerful tool for strengthening competitive positioning, enabling companies to access new markets, share risks, and innovate collaboratively.

The East India Company understood the value of partnerships centuries ago, forging alliances with local rulers to secure trade routes and resources. Modern companies, like Tesla, continue this tradition, partnering with Panasonic for battery production and leveraging these relationships to accelerate innovation and scale. Strategic partnerships allow businesses to combine strengths, mitigate weaknesses, and tackle challenges that would be insurmountable alone.[15]

Competitive positioning in supply chain management is more than keeping up with the competition—it's about leaving them behind. By focusing on market differentiation, developing core competencies, creating sustainable competitive advantages, and forging strategic partnerships, businesses can build supply chains that go way beyond *efficient* and become truly *exceptional*.

The most successful supply chains set trends when others are content to simply follow them. Whether it's Zara's speed, Amazon's logistics mastery, or Apple's ecosystem control, the lesson is clear: Competitive positioning isn't a single move; it's a strategy that plays out over time, redefining the rules of the game and securing a place at the top.

Risk Management

No matter how sophisticated your strategy, risk is inevitable. The COVID-19 pandemic, geopolitical tensions, and climate change highlight the importance of resilience in supply chain planning. Strategic risk management goes beyond having a plan B—it embeds resilience into the system itself.

This might mean diversifying supplier bases to avoid over-reliance on a single region, investing in automation to mitigate labor shortages, or redesigning supply chains to minimize environmental impact. Modern leaders also use advanced analytics to predict risks, from economic downturns to natural disasters, and adapt proactively.

Strategic vision in supply chain management is about more than surviving the present—it's about shaping the future. It's the difference between a Silk Road merchant simply reacting to shifting trade routes and an East India Company leader planning decades ahead to dominate entire markets.

Today's leaders have more tools, data, and technologies at their disposal than ever before. But success still depends on the same principles that guided the Romans, the merchants of the Silk Road, and the pioneers of global trade: Think ahead, balance risk with opportunity, and always be ready to adapt when things change.

As you design your supply chain empire, remember: The goal isn't merely to play the game—it's to shape the board, write the rules, and leave competitors scrambling to catch up.

THE FOUR STRATEGIC HORIZONS

Successful supply chain management addresses today's problems while also preparing for tomorrow's opportunities and challenges. The Four Strategic Horizons provide a framework for professionals to balance immediate needs with long-term aspirations, ensuring their supply chains are not only efficient and competitive but also resilient and sustainable.

Horizon 1:
Foundation (0–2 Years)

The first horizon stabilizes and strengthens the foundation of your supply chain. It addresses current inefficiencies, enhancing core capabilities, and responding to immediate competitive pressures. Think of this as the groundwork for everything else.

Core capabilities enhancement begins with investments in skills, tools, and processes that drive day-to-day operations. Process optimization eliminates bottlenecks and waste to ensure smoother workflows. This stage also demands an immediate competitive response to market pressures, whether through pricing strategies, service improvements, or faster delivery times.

Quick wins at this stage provide tangible results that boost morale and demonstrate progress. For example, a retailer might implement automated inventory management to reduce stockouts and overstock issues, delivering both cost savings and better customer satisfaction in the short term.

Horizon 2:
Evolution (2–5 Years)

Once the foundation is solid, the focus shifts to growth and expansion. Horizon 2 emphasizes forward-thinking initiatives that

Building the Foundation

Partnership Development
Establishing strategic partnerships to leverage synergies and resources.

Competitive Response
Increasing organizational capabilities to support growth and innovation.

Process Optimization
Integrating new technologies to enhance operations and competitiveness.

New Market Development
Exploring and entering new markets to expand and reach opportunities.

position the supply chain for future success. This is the stage where companies begin dreaming bigger, enter new markets, adopt emerging technologies, and expand their capabilities.

New market development may involve geographic expansion, targeting high-growth regions, or diversifying into adjacent industries. Technology adoption also plays a critical role by leveraging tools like AI, IoT, and blockchain to improve efficiency, transparency, and decision-making. Capability expansion is key to supporting growth, whether through new facilities, advanced analytics, or workforce development programs.

Partnership development also plays a central role in this phase. Building alliances with suppliers, distributors, and even competitors can unlock new opportunities and shared efficiencies. Companies like Walmart excel by working closely with suppliers to improve sustainability and reduce costs across the value chain.

Horizon 3: Revolution (5+ Years)

The third horizon marks the point when organizations stop *following* the rules and start *rewriting* them. This stage embraces disruptive innovation, creating entirely new markets and redefining industries. It's the realm of bold moves and Paradigm shifts—the kind that force competitors to scramble to catch up.

Disruptive innovation might involve developing a groundbreaking product or service that transforms the market. Think of Tesla's electric vehicles, which didn't simply compete with traditional cars but redefined what a car could be. Market creation follows as companies carve out new spaces for growth by addressing unmet needs or inventing new ones.

Paradigm shifts often accompany revolutionary changes as businesses challenge conventional thinking and introduce new ways of working. Industry redefinition ties it all together, as companies like Amazon and Alibaba combine e-commerce, logistics, and cloud computing into ecosystems that dominate the modern economy.

Horizon 4:
Sustainability

The final horizon is less about time frames and more about values. Sustainability is a necessity for businesses that want to grow in the twenty-first century. This horizon focuses on integrating environmental, social, and economic responsibility into the fabric of supply chain strategy.

Environmental impact is at the forefront, with companies aiming to reduce carbon emissions, minimize waste, and adopt

Industry Evolution and Revolution

Industry Definition and Redefinition
Redefining industry standards and practices through innovative changes.

Paradigm Shifts
Transforming fundamental beliefs and practices within an industry.

Market Creation
Developing new markets by identifying and fulfilling unmet needs.

Disruptive Innovation
Introducing groundbreaking technologies that challenge the status quo.

Achieving Sustainability

Circular Economy Integration
Implement systems that recycle and reuse resources.

Economic Sustainability
Ensure long-term financial viability through responsible practices.

Social Responsibility
Emphasize ethical practices and community engagement.

Environmental Impact
Focus on reducing pollution and preserving natural resources.

renewable energy sources. Social responsibility follows, ensuring ethical labor practices, community engagement, and diversity and inclusion across the value chain. Economic sustainability is equally important, balancing profitability with long-term resilience and stakeholder value.

Finally, circular economy integration represents the ultimate goal: designing supply chains that create zero waste, turning used products and materials into inputs for new production. Companies like Unilever and IKEA have led the charge here, embedding circular principles into their operations and setting the standard for sustainable supply chains.[16]

The Four Strategic Horizons offer supply chain professionals a road map to navigate the complexities of today's business environment while preparing for the challenges and opportunities of tomorrow. By addressing immediate needs, building for the future, embracing revolutionary ideas, and committing to sustainability, organizations can create supply chains that are both efficient and transformative.

In the end, the greatest supply chains adapt, innovate, and inspire. Whether you're strengthening your foundation, pushing the boundaries of innovation, or leading the charge for sustainability, the key lies in considering what your supply chain can do today while still focusing on what it can achieve tomorrow and beyond.

STRATEGIC TOOLS FOR MODERN TIMES

In a world of blockchain, AI, and machine learning, it's tempting to think of an exercise like a SWOT analysis as a relic of simpler times. But the truth is, this tried-and-true framework remains as relevant as ever. Why? Because it forces you to take a hard, honest look at your supply chain and assess what's working, what's not, and what could disrupt your plans. While the tools may have changed, the questions SWOT asks remain timeless.

Strengths: What You're Good At

Every successful supply chain has its superpowers. Maybe it's a lightning-fast logistics network, unbeatable supplier relationships, or a culture of innovation that ensures you're always ahead of the curve. Identifying these strengths isn't merely about patting yourself on the back; it's about leveraging them to maintain your competitive edge. Amazon's fulfillment centers, for example, demonstrate this strength, enabling them to promise—and deliver—two-day shipping at an unparalleled scale.

Weaknesses: What Keeps You Up at Night

Weaknesses are the cracks in the foundation that can lead to collapse if left unaddressed. Whether it's overreliance on a single supplier, outdated technology, or inefficiencies in last-mile delivery, every weakness represents a vulnerability. For example, during the early days of COVID-19, companies heavily dependent on just-in-time inventory systems discovered this the hard way when supply chain disruptions left shelves empty.

Opportunities: What Could Make You Rich

Opportunities are where growth happens. These might include expanding into new markets, adopting emerging technologies, or capitalizing on industry trends. The rise of e-commerce during the pandemic, for instance, was an opportunity that some companies seized with both hands, pivoting their supply chains to cater to changing consumer behaviors.

Threats: What Could Make You Vulnerable

Threats are the external forces that could derail your supply chain and, by extension, your business. From geopolitical tensions to cyber-attacks to disruptive start-ups, threats are everywhere—and ignoring them is not an option. The global semiconductor shortage is a case study in threats; it caught even the largest companies off guard, forcing many to halt production and rethink their sourcing strategies.[17]

Porter's Five Forces: Updated for Modern Times

Noted economist Michael Porter's Five Forces model has long been a staple of strategic planning, but like all frameworks, it needs updating to stay relevant. In today's fast-moving, TikTok-driven world, Porter's forces look a little different—but they're no less important.

1. Supplier Power

Suppliers hold immense power when what they offer is scarce or specialized. Just ask any automaker that struggled to secure semiconductors in 2021. When suppliers know they're holding all the cards, they can raise prices, cut supply, or prioritize other customers. Managing supplier relationships has never been more critical, and smart companies diversify their supplier base to mitigate this power.

2. Buyer Power

Today's consumers are more empowered than ever. With countless options just a click away, they hold the power to make or break your business. Whether they demand faster delivery, lower prices, or more sustainable practices, buyers can exert significant pressure on supply chains. The rise of

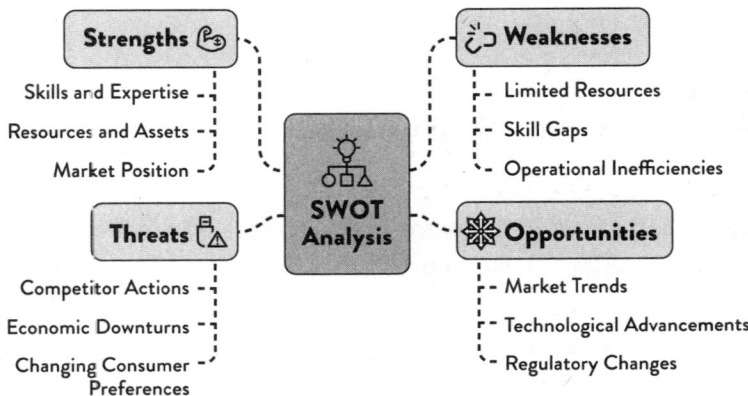

D2C brands only adds to this dynamic, giving customers even more control.

3. Competitive Rivalry

Competition is fierce, and innovation is hard to protect. The moment a company introduces a groundbreaking idea, competitors rush to replicate—and improve—it. Think of how quickly streaming services proliferated after Netflix's success. In supply chain terms, staying ahead requires constant evolution, whether through better technology, faster delivery, or superior customer experience.

4. New Entrants

Barriers to entry are lower than ever, thanks to technology and globalization. Start-ups with bold ideas and digital-first strategies can disrupt entire industries seemingly overnight. Airbnb, Peloton, and Uber are great examples.[18]

5. Substitutes

Substitutes are the wild card of competitive forces, replacing your product and rendering it obsolete. The shift from physical DVDs to streaming services is a classic example. In supply chain terms, this could mean the rise of localized 3D printing hubs, which could disrupt traditional manufacturing and logistics models by creating products on demand.

Frameworks like SWOT and Porter's Five Forces have stood the test of time for a reason: They help leaders think critically about their businesses in a structured way. But the value chain landscape is evolving rapidly, and these frameworks must be applied with a modern lens.

The key is not merely to identify strengths, weaknesses, opportunities, and threats—or to analyze competitive forces—but to act on these insights with agility and strategic intent.

After all, in today's world, the only constant is change. Whether you're facing a disruptive start-up, navigating geopolitical risks, or managing customer expectations, the ability to adapt and innovate separates the leaders from the laggards. As Michael Porter might put it today: The real challenge isn't identifying the forces. It's mastering them in a world that never stops changing.

STRATEGIC CHALLENGES IN THE MODERN ERA

Strategic challenges run the gamut from acting fast enough through ensuring reliability and navigating local and international considerations. Anticipating these challenges makes organizations more resilient in turbulent times.

Speed vs. Stability: The Constant Tug-of-War

Value chain professionals today face a balancing act, constantly juggling between speed and stability.

On one hand, markets are moving faster than ever, driven by evolving customer expectations, technological advancements, and hypercompetitive landscapes. On the other, the need for stability—ensuring the value chain remains resilient and reliable—has never been greater.

Balancing the two requires us to master:

Porter's Five Forces in Modern Context

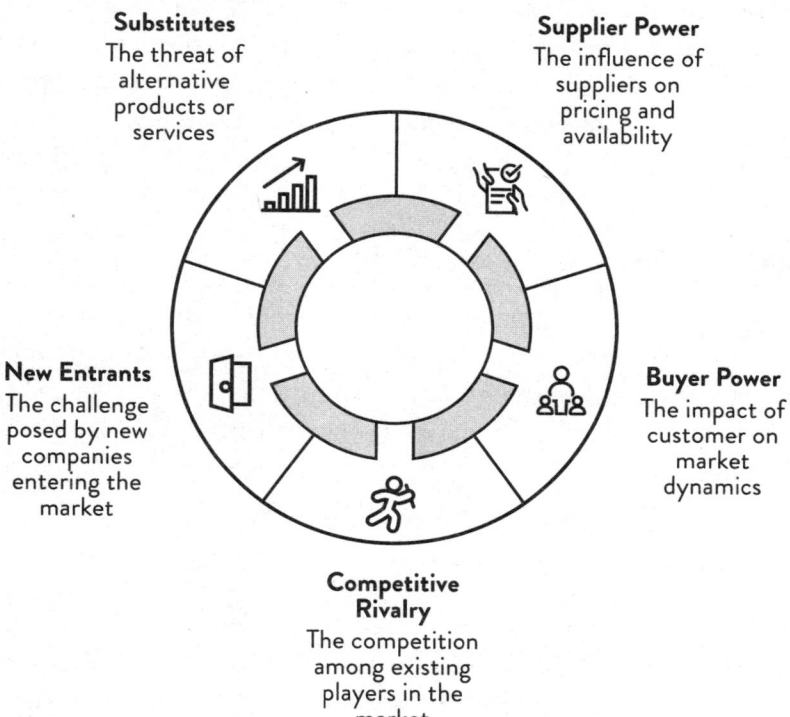

Substitutes
The threat of alternative products or services

Supplier Power
The influence of suppliers on pricing and availability

New Entrants
The challenge posed by new companies entering the market

Buyer Power
The impact of customer on market dynamics

Competitive Rivalry
The competition among existing players in the market

Fast Market Changes

In the digital age, demand can shift overnight. A viral TikTok video can turn an obscure product into a must-have sensation, leaving supply chains scrambling to keep up. Companies that prioritize speed, such as Zara and Amazon, excel by designing systems that allow them to respond quickly to these changes. However, moving too fast can also lead to overproduction, inefficiencies, and mistakes.

Technology Evolution

Advancements in AI, robotics, and IoT have enabled unprecedented speed in areas like inventory management, order fulfillment, and last-mile delivery. But these tools are only as good as their implementation. Relying too heavily on technology without proper oversight can create vulnerabilities, such as system failures or misaligned processes.

Customer Expectation Management

Today's customers demand faster delivery, real-time updates, and seamless experiences. Meeting these expectations requires prioritizing speed—but not at the expense of quality or reliability. Companies must strike a balance, ensuring that promises made are promises kept.

Risk Mitigation

Prioritizing speed can amplify risks, from supplier bottlenecks to transportation delays. Stability, on the other hand, ensures a more predictable and controlled operation, but it may come at the cost of agility. The modern value chain must find a way to do both—move fast without breaking under pressure.

Speed and stability must always be balanced so that an organization's adaptability, technology, customer service, and risk mitigation remain equally considered and addressed.

Think Globally, Act Locally: Panic Internationally

Global supply chains have long been hailed as marvels of efficiency, connecting businesses to resources, labor, and customers across the world. But as the pandemic and geopolitical tensions have shown, global operations can also be a source of vulnerability.

The challenge lies in balancing the efficiencies of globalization with the adaptability of local operations. This includes taking key factors into account, such as:

Local Market Requirements

Local markets have unique needs, from consumer preferences to delivery expectations. Companies like McDonald's excel at tailoring their products to local tastes, offering teriyaki burgers in Japan and plant-based McSpicy burgers in India.[19] Supply chains must be flexible enough to cater to these nuances while maintaining overall efficiency.

Global Efficiency

The economies of scale achieved through global operations are undeniable. By sourcing materials from low-cost regions or consolidating production, companies can keep costs down and remain competitive. However, this efficiency can be disrupted by events like trade wars or natural disasters, highlighting the need for contingency planning.

Cultural Considerations

Operating globally means navigating a complex web of cultural differences. From communication styles to negotiation tactics, cultural sensitivity is critical in building trust and maintaining strong relationships with international suppliers and partners.

Regulatory Compliance

Every country has its own set of rules and regulations, from labor laws to environmental standards. Navigating this patchwork of requirements is no small feat, but failing to do so can lead to fines, delays, or reputational damage. Companies like Unilever have mastered the art of regulatory navigation by ensuring compliance without sacrificing efficiency.

In the twenty-first century, organizations have become increasingly vulnerable both locally and internationally. Addressing these factors helps to mitigate that vulnerability.

Innovation vs. Reliability: Blending Old and New

The tension between innovation and reliability is a classic dilemma. While innovation drives growth, attracts customers, and keeps companies ahead of the competition, it also introduces uncertainty. Reliability, meanwhile, ensures customer satisfaction and operational consistency but can sometimes hinder progress.

Adopting Disruptive Technology

Companies that embrace innovation often reap significant rewards, as Tesla has shown with its electric vehicles and autonomous driving technologies. However, adopting disruptive technologies comes with risks, including implementation challenges, stakeholder resistance, and unexpected side effects.

Process Stability

Reliability requires stable, repeatable processes that ensure consistent outcomes. For value chains, this means meeting delivery promises, maintaining quality, and avoiding disruptions. Companies like Toyota have built their reputations on this principle, using lean manufacturing to achieve both stability and efficiency.[20]

Customer Satisfaction

Customers want the best of both worlds: cutting-edge innovation and dependable service. Striking this balance is critical. Apple, for instance, excels by introducing groundbreaking products while maintaining a reputation for reliability and strong customer support.

Employee Adaptation

Innovation often demands significant changes to workflows, tools, and skill sets. Ensuring employees are equipped to adapt is essential for long-term success. This means investing in training, fostering a culture of continuous learning, and addressing resistance to change.

Balancing speed and stability, global and local priorities, and innovation and reliability is the ultimate challenge for modern value chain teams. These opposing forces require adequate change management and rigorous processes to ensure effective communications and adoption.

The most successful companies don't choose one factor over the other. Instead, they master the art of balance. They innovate without sacrificing quality, expand globally while honoring local needs, and move fast while staying grounded. In a world of constant change, this ability to navigate complexity sets organizations apart.

THE STRATEGY IMPLEMENTATION BLUEPRINT

A grand vision is only as good as its execution. Whether you're building a supply chain empire or fine-tuning existing operations, strategy implementation requires careful planning, clear communication, and an unwavering focus on the end goal. The Strategy

Implementation Blueprint lays out three steps for turning strategic vision into actionable results, ensuring every move is deliberate, efficient, and impactful.

Step 1:
Vision, Goals, and Timeline

The foundation of any successful strategy is a well-defined vision. It begins with clear direction-setting, ensuring that all stakeholders understand the overarching goals and objectives. Without clarity, even the most innovative strategy can falter under misaligned priorities.

Stakeholder alignment is equally crucial. From C-suite executives to frontline workers, to suppliers and customers, everyone must pull in the same direction. This requires consistent communication, collaboration, and buy-in from key players to champion the strategy at every level of the organization.

Once the vision is clear and everyone is aligned, the next priority is articulating exactly which goals to achieve. These goals must be specific, measurable, and tied to tangible outcomes, whether that means achieving a 10 percent reduction in logistics costs or expanding into three new markets within five years.

Finally, a timeline must be established to ensure progress is tracked and milestones met, creating accountability and momentum throughout the implementation process.

Step 2:
Resource Allocation

Every strategy lives or dies by its resources. Even the most brilliant vision cannot succeed without the proper allocation of people, technology, and capital. Capital investment comes first: Adequate funding must be allocated to strategic initiatives, whether that means building new facilities, upgrading technology, or hiring specialized talent.

Talent development is another critical component. As supply chains become more complex, the need for skilled professionals who can manage AI systems, negotiate with global suppliers, and lead cross-functional teams has never been greater. Companies must invest in training, mentorship, and recruitment to build a workforce capable of executing the strategy.

Technology acquisition is equally important. From predictive analytics platforms to automated warehouse systems, the right tools can transform operations, driving efficiency and innovation. Finally, market development ensures that resources are directed toward expanding market reach, whether by entering high-growth regions, launching new product lines, or forging strategic partnerships.

Step 3:
Execution Framework

With the vision and resources in place, the focus shifts to execution. An effective execution framework begins with project prioritization, ensuring that the most critical initiatives receive the necessary attention and resources. Not all projects are created equal, and leaders must identify which efforts will drive the greatest impact in the shortest time frame.

Progress monitoring is essential to keep implementation on track. This involves regular check-ins, real-time data analysis, and reporting mechanisms that highlight both achievements and roadblocks. When challenges arise—as they inevitably will—adjustment mechanisms need to be in place to enable quick, effective course corrections and minimize disruption.

Finally, success metrics provide a clear measure of progress and impact. Whether they are on-time delivery rates, cost savings, or market share growth, these metrics ensure accountability and celebrate milestones, reinforcing the team's commitment to the strategy.

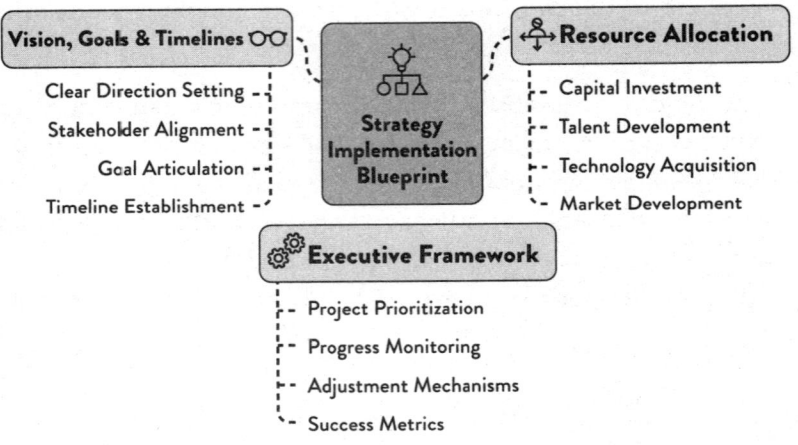

Vision, Goals & Timelines
- Clear Direction Setting
- Stakeholder Alignment
- Goal Articulation
- Timeline Establishment

Strategy Implementation Blueprint

Resource Allocation
- Capital Investment
- Talent Development
- Technology Acquisition
- Market Development

Executive Framework
- Project Prioritization
- Progress Monitoring
- Adjustment Mechanisms
- Success Metrics

THE BOTTOM LINE: FORESIGHT AS A MULTIPLIER

Strategic vision in modern value chain management is like playing three-dimensional chess while riding a bicycle—it requires balance, foresight, and the ability to adapt when things don't go as planned. The merchants of the Silk Road had to contend with bandits and sandstorms; today's professionals face chip shortages, cyberattacks, and fluctuating consumer demand. Different challenges, same need for strategic thinking.

Just as the Silk Road merchants didn't build their networks overnight, modern supply chain strategy requires patience, persistence, and the ability to see opportunities where others see obstacles. Think of the ancient metallurgists who forged Damascus steel—its exact composition remained a mystery for centuries, copied but never quite matched.[21] Strategy works the same way: The pattern may be imitated, but the strength lies in what others can't see—the process, the discipline, the adaptability under pressure.

The key is to think big, start small, move fast, and always keep one eye on the horizon. In the end, strategy isn't only about playing the game better than everyone else; it's about changing the game itself.

CHAPTER 4

THE ART OF NEGOTIATION

Imagine the year 1615: The East India Company, only fifteen years after its formation in 1600 with a royal charter, had already laid the groundwork for what would become one of the most formidable global value chains in history.[1] The stakes were monumental. On the one hand, they were negotiating with Mughal Emperor Jahangir for the rights to trade in India—a land rich in spices, textiles, and opulent resources. On the other, they were dealing with fierce competitors like the Dutch East India Company, which already controlled the lucrative spice trade in Southeast Asia.[2]

The results of these negotiations shaped the fortunes of nations. The East India Company secured permission to establish a factory—a trading post—in Surat, a key port city, in exchange for a lucrative annual tribute to the Mughal emperor.[3] This deal laid the foundation for British dominance in India.

The tribute was a small price to pay for access to markets worth millions—an astronomical sum at the time. By the mid-seventeenth century, trade between Britain and India alone accounted for a significant portion of England's GDP, with spices and textiles fetching margins of 300 percent or more in European markets.[4]

Fast-forward to 1661, and the stakes had risen exponentially. The Company negotiated exclusive rights to mint its own currency in Bombay—modern-day Mumbai—granted as part of a dowry when the Portuguese ceded the island to England.[5] This financial autonomy allowed the East India Company to streamline transactions and control trade flows, further solidifying its power. In today's terms, the wealth generated by these deals equates to billions of dollars annually.[6]

These negotiations weren't merely about short-term wins; they were calculated moves to dominate value chains and create enduring systems of influence. But they were not without costs. The exorbitant wealth extracted from India and other colonies came at the price of social upheaval and exploitation—a stark reminder that negotiation strategies must account for long-term sustainability and equity.

MODERN NEGOTIATIONS: A DIFFERENT BATTLEFIELD

Today, value chain negotiations may not involve kings and empires, but the stakes remain high. Instead of negotiating for exclusive trade rights, businesses compete for access to critical resources like semiconductors, rare earth metals, and skilled labor. The sums involved are staggering. A modern semiconductor fabrication plant, for instance, costs more than $10 billion, with companies like TSMC (Taiwan Semiconductor Manufacturing Company) and Intel leveraging their dominance to dictate terms to global buyers.[7]

In 2021, automakers worldwide lost an estimated $110 billion in revenue due to semiconductor shortages, highlighting the staggering cost of failing to secure favorable supplier agreements.[8] Negotiations in such a landscape are no longer only about price; they're about priority. When a supplier has limited capacity, being first in line can make or break a company's quarterly or annual earnings.

The lessons from history remain relevant: Relationships matter, power dynamics shift, and successful negotiation requires a blend of strategy, leverage, and foresight. Just as the East India Company used its navy to secure trade routes, today's companies use data analytics, market intelligence, and strategic partnerships to ensure they remain competitive.

THE FOUR PILLARS OF MODERN NEGOTIATION

We all negotiate every day. Anyone with a toddler understands you don't always get what you want, and coercive tactics can easily backfire. Focus on the following pillars to improve your outcomes.

Pillar #1:
Power Dynamics

Negotiation begins and ends with power. The balance—or imbalance—of power dictates terms, timelines, and outcomes. In the world of value chains, power dynamics shift constantly, influenced by factors such as market demand, supplier strength, buyer leverage, and geopolitical events. Understanding who needs whom more is essential to develop an effective negotiation strategy.

Modern Power Considerations:

There are several factors that drive the shifting balance of power in value chains:

Market Position—Are You Apple . . . or "Generic Tech Company 7"?

Market leaders wield significant power in negotiations due to their scale, brand strength, and financial resources. Apple, for instance, exercises immense leverage over its suppliers. By placing massive orders for custom components, Apple can negotiate favorable prices, delivery schedules, and exclusivity agreements. In 2020, Apple spent $58 billion with its top two hundred suppliers, a figure no supplier can afford to ignore.[9]

In contrast, smaller companies, such as "Generic Tech Company 7," often are at the mercy of their suppliers, forced to accept less-favorable terms due to a lack of purchasing volume or brand clout.

The lesson? A strong market position translates into better leverage—and often, better deals. For smaller firms, however, cultivating relationships and partnerships is critical for offsetting weaker leverage.

Supply Alternatives—Can You Get It Elsewhere . . . or Are You Stuck?

The more alternatives you have, the more power you wield. During that global semiconductor shortage, automakers like Ford and GM suffered severe disruptions because they relied heavily on a handful of chip manufacturers. In contrast, companies with diversified supplier networks—such as Toyota—fared much better, as they could pivot to alternative suppliers.[10]

This principle is equally true in smaller-scale negotiations. If your supplier knows you have no other options, they hold the upper hand. Conversely, if you can source the same product or service elsewhere, you can negotiate more assertively.

Demand Leverage—How Badly Do They Need Your Business?

Suppliers are businesses, too, and they depend on steady demand to survive. When a customer represents a significant portion of their revenue, the balance of power shifts toward the buyer. Walmart, for example, uses its status as one of the world's largest retailers to negotiate favorable terms with suppliers. By guaranteeing high-volume purchases, Walmart secures lower prices and priority service.[11]

However, this dynamic can flip when demand exceeds supply. For example, during the pandemic, suppliers of personal protective equipment (PPE) dictated terms to desperate buyers who had no leverage. In such cases, even contracts could not override force majeure events, leaving buyers in vulnerable positions.

Time Pressure—Is This a "Nice to Have" or a "Need It Yesterday"?

Time is often the ultimate arbiter of power in negotiations. If one party is under significant time pressure, they're more likely to make concessions. A supplier who knows you need materials urgently can hold firm on pricing, knowing you're unlikely to walk away. Conversely, if you have the luxury of time, you can explore alternatives, push for better terms, and even walk away if the deal doesn't meet your needs.

In 2021, shipping delays caused by port congestion created significant time pressure for retailers preparing for the holiday season. At the Port of Los Angeles, for instance, fifty to sixty ships often waited offshore to unload. Those who could afford to expedite shipments via airfreight gained an advantage, while others were forced to pay premiums to move product through the port and secure expedited trucking to ensure on-time delivery. Some retailers missed the boat—literally—and had to wait until the next holiday season.[12]

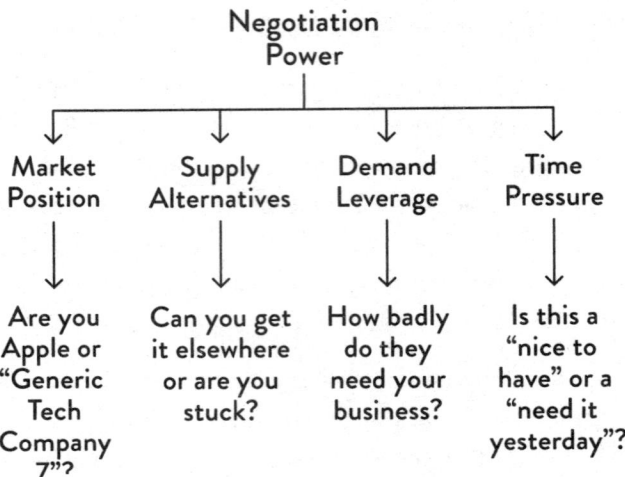

Historical Perspective

Power dynamics in negotiation are nothing new. During the seventeenth century, The East India Company frequently leveraged its status as a high-volume buyer to negotiate favorable terms with local rulers and traders. Its dominance in the global spice trade allowed it to dictate prices and shipping terms, often to the detriment of local economies.

However, the Company also faced situations where power was out of its hands. When Mughal Emperor Aurangzeb imposed higher taxes on British merchants in the late 1600s, the Company had no choice but to comply, as the Mughals controlled access to critical markets and resources.[13] This historical example underscores the importance of understanding and adapting to shifting power dynamics in negotiations.

Negotiation power isn't static. It's a fluid, ever-changing force that depends on market conditions, relationships, and strategic positioning. By understanding the factors that influence power dynamics, value chain professionals can navigate negotiations with confidence, securing deals that benefit their organizations while building stronger, more resilient partnerships.

Ultimately, the key to mastering power dynamics is preparation. Know your strengths, understand the other party's weaknesses, and always have a backup plan—because in negotiation, as in chess, the player with the most options usually wins.

Pillar #2:
Value Creation

Negotiation is often perceived as a game of numbers, where the goal is securing the lowest price or the biggest paycheck. But in modern value chain management, value creation goes far beyond the price tag. Today's successful negotiations focus on building partnerships that deliver long-term benefits, from reducing total costs to fostering innovation. True value isn't only about what you pay; it's about what you gain.

Modern Value Creation Elements

Creating value comes down to a handful of important factors that shape effective agreements:

Total Cost of Ownership (TCO)—Thinking Beyond the Sticker Price

When negotiating supply agreements, the focus shouldn't be limited to the up-front cost. TCO accounts for all expenses associated with a product or service over its life cycle, including maintenance, disposal, and downtime. A lower-cost component might seem like a bargain, but if it results in higher repair costs or production delays, it could end up costing far more in the long run.[14]

Quality Guarantees—Because Cheap Doesn't Always Mean Good

Quality is a cornerstone of value creation. A product that fails to meet standards not only disrupts operations but also can damage customer trust and brand reputation. This is why modern negotiations often include quality guarantees, such as detailed specifications, testing protocols, and penalty clauses for noncompliance.

Service Levels—The Unsung Hero of Supply Chain Success

Great products are meaningless without reliable service. Service levels encompass everything from on-time delivery to responsive customer support, and they're often the differentiator in competitive markets. Negotiations that include clear service-level agreements (SLAs) help ensure that suppliers meet performance benchmarks, fostering trust and minimizing disruptions.

Innovation Sharing—A Win-Win Approach

In today's fast-moving markets, innovation is a key driver of success. Forward-thinking companies use negotiations as an opportunity to foster collaboration and share ideas with their partners. This might involve codeveloping new products, streamlining production processes, or leveraging new technologies to improve efficiency.

Risk Sharing—Navigating Uncertainty Together

Supply chains are inherently risky, from fluctuating demand to geopolitical instability. Modern negotiations often include risk-sharing provisions, ensuring both parties work together to mitigate potential disruptions. This might involve shared inventory costs, flexible payment terms, or joint investments in backup facilities.

Modern Value Creation Elements

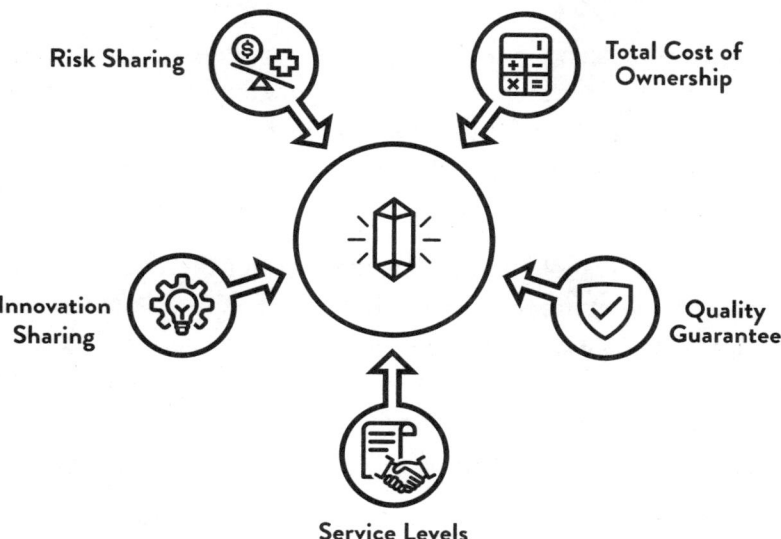

Historical Perspective

The concept of value creation isn't new. During the seventeenth century, the East India Company negotiated deals that went far beyond price. By offering local rulers access to European goods and technologies, the Company secured trade rights that fueled its dominance. However, its failure to balance value with fairness ultimately led to backlash, highlighting the importance of equitable agreements.

Value creation is the heart of modern negotiations. By focusing on elements like TCO, quality, service, innovation, and risk sharing, companies can build partnerships that deliver far more than financial savings.

In today's complex value chains, success depends on creating value that benefits both parties—because when both sides win, the relationship and the results speak for themselves.

Pillar #3:
Relationship Management

Picture the bustling Silk Road at its height—a vast network stretching over four thousand miles, connecting empires, cultures, and merchants. At its core, the system relied not just on the movement of goods, but on the relationships that enabled such a complex network to function.

From the camel herders navigating treacherous mountain passes to the traders in bustling bazaars, the Silk Road was successfully sustained because of strong interpersonal connections, trust, and shared goals. It was far more than a trade route; it was a network of human relationships.

In the modern world, the lessons of the Silk Road remain just as relevant. Value chain relationships are the bedrock of success, stability, and innovation.

Mastering relationships in business might sound terrifying, especially if you're a natural introvert who enjoys nothing more than spending a Sunday afternoon all alone, curled up on the sofa with a cup of coffee and a fascinating book about value chains. Even if that describes you, relationship management doesn't have to be scary. It boils down to attending to a handful of key elements, including:

Long-Term Partnership Development

Merchants on the Silk Road didn't succeed by making onetime deals. Relationships were nurtured over years, with traders offering consistent quality and fair terms to ensure repeat business. Long-term partnerships provided stability in a volatile trade environment, where trust was often the only assurance of safety and fairness.

Build Trust

Imagine a trader sending precious silk or spices across hundreds of miles with only a verbal agreement. Trust was the currency of the Silk Road, built on shared success, reputation, and word-of-mouth credibility. Breaking trust could mean financial ruin—or worse, exclusion from the network.

Modern value chains demand the same level of trust. Transparency, consistency, and integrity are critical.

Align Cultures

The Silk Road was more than a trade route; it was a melting pot of cultures. Merchants adapted to local customs, languages, and traditions to build connections and gain trust. A Persian trader learned Chinese etiquette, while an Indian merchant understood Roman preferences, ensuring smooth transactions.

Today, businesses that operate globally must prioritize cultural alignment. Understanding local norms, values, and expectations is crucial for building partnerships.

Solve Problems Jointly

The Silk Road wasn't without challenges. Bandits, storms, and political upheaval threatened the flow of goods. Traders often collaborated to solve problems, pooling resources or adjusting routes to overcome obstacles.

Modern value chains face their own crises, from natural disasters to supply disruptions. Strong relationships enable joint problem-solving, where partners work together to find solutions.

Crisis Management Protocols

When a caravan broke down or a route became unsafe, Silk Road merchants relied on established protocols and trusted allies to navigate the crisis. Modern value chains operate on similar principles, where preestablished crisis management frameworks ensure swift and effective responses.

Effective Relationship Management

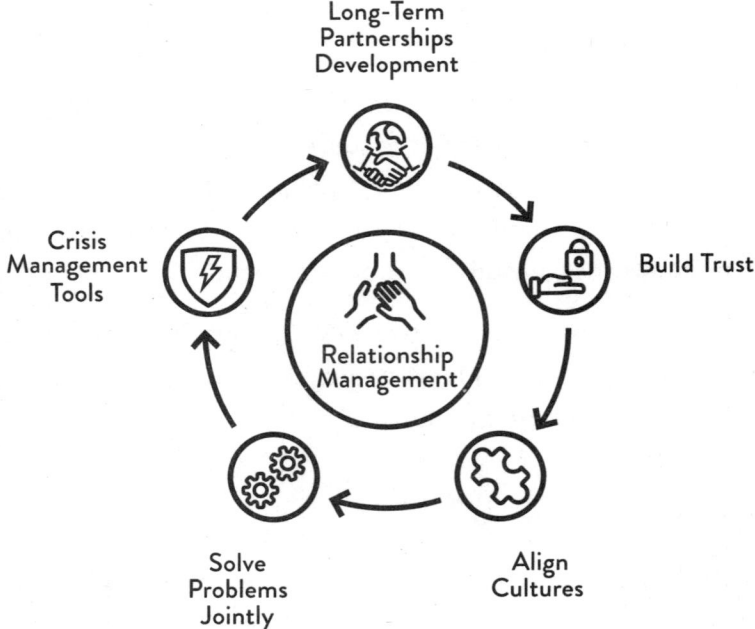

Historical Perspective

The Silk Road teaches us that strong relationships can span cultures, languages, and geographies, creating networks that endure for centuries. But it also warns us of the risks of neglecting those relationships. When trust eroded—whether through exploitation or broken promises—trade routes faltered, and empires faced oblivion.

The Silk Road lasted because its merchants understood that business is personal. Relationships were the true infrastructure of the route, ensuring that goods, knowledge, and culture flowed seamlessly across continents.

Modern value chains may rely on algorithms and automation, but the principles of relationship management remain the same. Trust, alignment, and collaboration keep the wheels turning, even in the face of disruption. Because whether you're trading silk or semiconductors, the strength of your relationships determines the strength of your value chain.

Pillar #4: Risk Mitigation

If ever there was a company that lived by the maxim "Anything that can go wrong, will go wrong," it was the East India Company. Operating during the seventeenth and eighteenth centuries, this global trading powerhouse faced every imaginable risk: shipwrecks, piracy, supply shortages, political upheaval, and even outright wars. Yet the Company proliferated, becoming one of history's most profitable enterprises. How did it survive? Through meticulous risk mitigation strategies that continue to offer valuable lessons today.

There are several essential components when mitigating risk. These include:

Contract Terms and Conditions—The Devil Is in the Details

The East India Company's contracts were legendary for their detail and scope. These documents accounted for everything from shipment delivery timelines to financial penalties for late arrivals. By locking in clear terms and conditions, the Company minimized ambiguity and ensured that both parties understood their obligations.

Modern contracts follow the same principle, providing clear, detailed terms that protect businesses from misunderstandings and disputes. For example, supplier contracts in the tech industry often specify penalties for late deliveries, ensuring that high-stakes operations like cell phone manufacturing aren't derailed by delays.[15] Time is money, after all.

Performance Guarantees—A Promise Is a Promise

The company relied heavily on performance guarantees to ensure reliability. Captains of the Company ships, for instance, were required to deliver cargo intact or face significant financial penalties. These guarantees incentivized compliance and minimized losses.

Today, performance guarantees remain a cornerstone of risk mitigation. Businesses frequently negotiate SLAs with suppliers, outlining specific performance metrics—such as on-time delivery rates or defect thresholds—and include penalties for noncompliance.

Exit Clauses—Know When to Walk Away

With trade routes spanning continents and decades-long partnerships, the Company understood the need for flexibility. Many of its agreements included exit clauses that allowed the Company to pivot if a supplier failed to meet expectations or if geopolitical circumstances changed.

In modern value chains, exit clauses are equally critical. Whether it's shifting suppliers during a trade war or exiting a partnership due to quality issues, these provisions provide the freedom to adapt without incurring excessive penalties.

Force Majeure Provisions—Planning for the Unplannable

A force majeure event is an external shock that sits outside the reasonable control of any single organization and materially disrupts the flow of goods, services, labor, capital, or information across a value chain. From monsoons in the Indian Ocean to naval blockades in Europe, the Company faced a constant barrage of uncontrollable events. Force majeure clauses in contracts protected both parties from liability when disasters struck, ensuring that neither party bore undue responsibility for events beyond their control.

These provisions are just as relevant today. The COVID-19 pandemic, for instance, highlighted the importance of force majeure clauses, as countless businesses invoked them to navigate disruptions in supply, labor, and logistics.[16]

Intellectual Property Protection—Safeguarding the Crown Jewels

The East India Company fiercely protected its trade secrets, particularly its knowledge of markets, pricing, and logistics. This intellectual property (IP) was critical to maintaining its competitive edge. When the Company's textile designs were copied by competitors, it responded by innovating new patterns and techniques to stay ahead.

Modern businesses face even greater IP risks, particularly in industries like technology and pharmaceuticals. Negotiating robust IP protection clauses ensures that valuable innovations are safeguarded, preventing competitors from gaining an unfair advantage.

Contractual Considerations

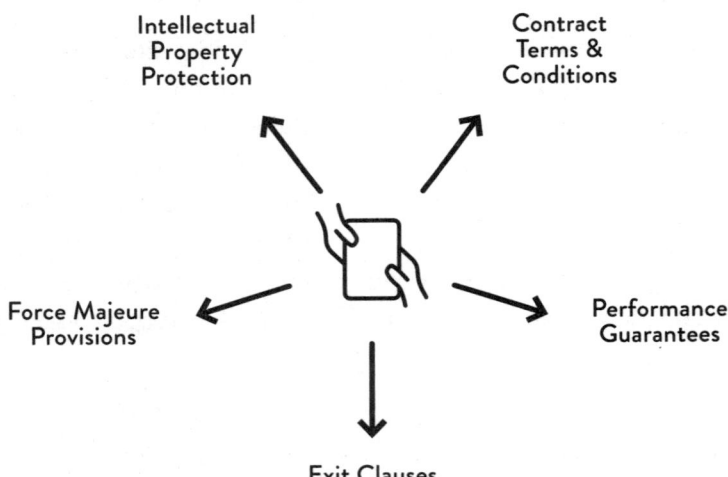

Intellectual Property Protection

Contract Terms & Conditions

Force Majeure Provisions

Performance Guarantees

Exit Clauses

Historical Perspective

Risk mitigation wasn't merely a strategy for the East India Company; it was a necessity. Every ship that set sail represented a massive investment, and every trade route carried the potential for conflict. Yet, by embedding risk management into its contracts, operations, and relationships, the Company navigated these challenges with remarkable success.

Risk is an inevitable part of value chain management, but it doesn't have to be debilitating. By adopting robust mitigation strategies—detailed contracts, performance guarantees, exit clauses, force majeure provisions, and IP protections—businesses can navigate uncertainty with confidence.

Just as the East India Company braved storms, wars, and political intrigue to dominate global trade, modern value chain professionals can overcome their own challenges by preparing for the worst while striving for the best. In the end, risk isn't something to fear—it's something to manage.

MODERN NEGOTIATION CHALLENGES

I have a teenager. He needed a new car and was adamant he was going to negotiate a better deal than I could. Of course, his mother knows nothing. As I struggled with his independence, I knew a plan was required to help him navigate this educational opportunity.

First, I needed to determine the lowest possible price I thought the vehicle was worth. I made out a bank draft for that amount. I then took out cash to cover the delta between what *I* thought the car was worth and what *he* thought it was worth.

I then sat him down and explained that he could keep any cash he negotiated off what he thought the car was worth. No strings attached. Suddenly he was very excited to enter negotiations with a renewed goal in mind. He negotiated for the car, purchased it, and—surprise, surprise—negotiated a much better deal. He managed to keep 75 percent of the cash and now loves to negotiate nearly everything with me.

Your results may vary.

Virtual Negotiations—When You Can't Read the Room Because There Isn't One

Virtual negotiations have become an indispensable part of modern business, driven by the rise of globalization, remote work, and advancements in technology. Yet the absence of nonverbal cues, the complexity of time zones, and the potential for cultural missteps present unique challenges. Despite these hurdles, virtual negotiations are increasingly proving their value, enabling businesses to save time, cut costs, and collaborate across continents.

Drawing inspiration from historical practices, such as the Silk Road's use of intermediaries and detailed correspondence, today's virtual negotiations leverage technology to achieve clarity and efficiency. But like traders from centuries past, modern negotiators must prepare meticulously to ensure success.

Challenges

Though convenient and effective at bringing people together, virtual negotiations aren't without their unique challenges, including:

Limited Nonverbal Cues

Silk Road traders often relied on face-to-face meetings to establish trust and finalize agreements. Without these interactions, they risked misjudging a partner's honesty or intentions, leading to financial losses or damaged reputations.

Nonverbal communication—such as body language and facial expressions—can account for more than 50 percent of human communication. The absence of these cues in virtual settings can lead to misunderstandings and missed opportunities to gauge emotions and intentions.[17]

Technology Issues

Technical glitches can disrupt the flow of negotiations, causing frustration and delays. From audio dropouts to platform incompatibility, these issues are especially challenging when the stakes are high.

Time Zone Coordination

Coordinating across multiple time zones can result in fatigue and misaligned schedules, affecting productivity and engagement. This is particularly challenging for global teams spanning continents.

Traders on the Silk Road had to wait weeks or months to align schedules with partners, as travel times varied greatly. Today, the challenge is compressed into hours but remains just as complex.

Cultural Nuances in Virtual Settings

Cultural differences can lead to misinterpretation, especially in virtual settings where subtle cues are harder to detect. This makes understanding cultural norms and expectations critical to successful negotiations.

Solutions

Fortunately, none of these challenges are insurmountable. They simply require some extra attention to a few key areas:

Enhanced Preparation

Preparation is even more critical in virtual negotiations. This includes researching participants' cultural norms, testing technology platforms, and preparing detailed agendas.

The East India Company relied on written correspondence, including detailed negotiation terms, to overcome the challenges of long-distance communication. These documents were meticulously crafted to avoid ambiguity—a lesson modern businesses should apply to virtual negotiations.

Clear Communication Protocols

Establishing structured communication norms reduces the risk of misinterpretation. This includes setting clear agendas, summarizing key points, and explicitly inviting feedback.

Companies like Zoom and Microsoft Teams have built-in tools to facilitate communication, such as hand-raising features and real-time transcription.

Regular Check-Ins

Virtual negotiations can be exhausting, especially when spanning time zones. Scheduling short breaks and regular check-ins keeps participants engaged and aligned.

Documentation Discipline

Comprehensive documentation is vital for ensuring alignment and preventing disputes. Meeting minutes, action items, and summaries should be promptly shared.

Silk Road traders recorded agreements on parchment, while the Romans recorded them on clay tablets, ensuring that both parties had a clear record. Today, businesses use digital tools like DocuSign and Google Docs for real-time collaboration and secure recordkeeping.

Virtual negotiations have redefined how businesses interact, offering efficiency and convenience while presenting unique challenges. By learning from historical practices like the detailed records of Silk Road traders and the disciplined correspondence of the East India Company, modern negotiators can adapt and succeed in virtual environments.

Virtual Communication

Solutions ⟨VS⟩ Challenges

	Solutions		Challenges
☑	Enhanced Preparation	? !	Limited Non-Verbal Cues
👥	Clear Communication Protocols	⚡	Technology Issues
📅	Regular Check-Ins	🕐	Time Zone Coordination
📝	Documentation Discipline	🌐	Cultural Nuances

With enhanced preparation, clear communication, and robust documentation, virtual negotiations can be as effective as traditional in-person meetings—if not more so. After all, the tools have changed, but the principles of trust, clarity, and collaboration remain timeless.

Multiparty Negotiations—Herding Cats While Juggling

Multiparty negotiations can be difficult because they require more of everything—resources, time, research, and collaboration. The more stakeholders involved, the more complex the process becomes. Every party has unique interests, priorities, and pressures, requiring negotiators to align competing agendas, build coalitions, and distribute value in ways that maintain coopera-tion. From the coalition building of the East India Company to the complex trading networks of the Silk Road, history offers valuable lessons for navigating multiparty negotiations.

Consider the following when entering into multiparty negotia-tions:

Stakeholder Management
Managing multiple stakeholders requires an understanding of each party's objectives, constraints, and decision-making processes. Transparency and clear communication are essen-tial in preventing misunderstandings and conflicts.

In the eighteenth century, the East India Company nego-tiated with local rulers, tribal leaders, and other European powers to secure trade rights in India. For example, the 1765 Treaty of Allahabad between the East India Company and the Mughal Empire granted the Company tax collection rights in Bengal, Bihar, and Orissa—one of the most lucrative agree-ments in the Company's history.[18]

Interest Alignment
Identifying common interests among parties is the founda-tion of multiparty negotiations. By emphasizing shared goals, negotiators can foster collaboration and reduce friction.

Along the Silk Road, merchants often pooled resources to secure safe passage through dangerous regions. By aligning their interests—avoiding theft and ensuring timely delivery—they created a cooperative framework that benefited all parties.

Coalition Building
In complex negotiations, building coalitions with aligned parties can strengthen your position and create leverage.

However, maintaining these alliances requires trust and careful management of competing priorities.

The East India Company often built coalitions with smaller local rulers to counterbalance powerful adversaries. By offering trade incentives or military support, the Company secured strategic alliances that expanded its influence.

Complex Value Distribution
Dividing value among multiple parties is one of the most challenging aspects of multiparty negotiations. The key is creating value rather than merely dividing it, ensuring each party feels that their interests are addressed.

Roman Empire trade agreements often included provisions for shared profits, resource exchanges, and mutual protection. These agreements balanced the needs of Roman merchants with those of local communities, fostering long-term partnerships.

Strategies for Success

In multiparty negotiations, always be prepared for things to go sideways. Here are some strategies to keep in mind for navigating better outcomes:

Map Stakeholders and Interests
Create a detailed map of all parties involved, outlining their goals, priorities, and potential conflicts. This allows you to anticipate objections and craft proposals that address diverse needs.

Facilitate Open Communication
Establish clear communication channels to ensure all parties are heard and misunderstandings are minimized. Virtual tools

like collaborative platforms can streamline discussions in global negotiations.

Focus on Value Creation
Shift the conversation from dividing the pie to growing it. Explore creative solutions that generate additional value for all parties, such as joint ventures, shared investments, or long-term partnerships.

Leverage Coalitions Strategically
Build alliances with aligned parties to strengthen your position. However, be mindful to maintain balance and trust within the coalition to avoid internal conflicts.

Prepare for Iterative Discussions
Multiparty negotiations often require multiple rounds of discussion to refine proposals and address concerns. Be patient and prepared for a dynamic process.

Multiparty negotiations require the finesse of a diplomat, the strategy of a chess master, and the patience of a monk. By focusing on stakeholder alignment, coalition building, and value creation, negotiators can navigate even the most complex discussions and achieve mutually beneficial outcomes.

CROSS-CULTURAL NEGOTIATIONS

Negotiating across cultures is like navigating a maze where the rules of engagement change at every turn. A simple yes might mean agreement, a polite no, or an invitation to further discussion. Whether you're trading silk on the ancient Silk Road or finalizing a joint venture with a multinational corporation, understanding cultural norms, communication styles, and decision-making processes is critical to success.

Key Elements

In Japan, business negotiations often emphasize harmony and group consensus, with indirect communication and long deliberation periods. In contrast, American businesses prioritize efficiency and direct communication, sometimes leading to friction if cultural differences aren't acknowledged. Here are some additional recommendations for negotiating cross-culturally:

Cultural Awareness
Cultural differences impact how negotiations are initiated, conducted, and closed. Awareness of these nuances allows negotiators to avoid misunderstandings and build stronger relationships.

Along the Silk Road, traders learned to adapt their negotiation styles based on the cultures they encountered. In Persia, merchants prioritized hospitality and formalities before discussing terms, while in central Asia, direct bargaining was more common.

Communication Styles
Verbal and nonverbal communication styles vary widely across cultures. Some cultures value directness, while others rely on subtlety and implication. Misinterpreting these signals can derail negotiations.

Pay attention to both spoken and unspoken cues. When in doubt, ask for clarification to ensure mutual understanding.

Decision-Making Processes

Different cultures approach decision-making in unique ways. Some emphasize hierarchy and centralized authority, while others prioritize consensus and collaboration. Understanding these processes can prevent frustration and delays.

The East India Company encountered hierarchical decision-making when negotiating with Indian rulers, where agreements often required approval from multiple advisers or family members. This understanding allowed the Company to adjust its timelines and strategies.

Relationship-Building Norms

In many cultures, trust and relationships are a prerequisite for business. Rushing into negotiations without establishing rapport can be seen as disrespectful or opportunistic.

Traders on the Silk Road often exchanged gifts, shared meals, and engaged in lengthy discussions before broaching business topics. These rituals established trust and mutual respect.

Strategies for Success

Cross-cultural negotiation is a dance between hard and soft skills. These strategies focus on the soft skills that can make or break any deal.

Research Cultural Norms

Before entering negotiations, study the cultural background of your counterparts. This includes understanding their communication preferences, business etiquette, and decision-making styles.

Adapt Your Style

Flexibility is crucial. Adjust your approach to align with the other party's expectations, whether that means adopting a more formal tone, prioritizing relationship building, or allowing more time for deliberation.

Leverage Local Expertise

Engage local advisers or cultural consultants to provide insights and bridge gaps. These experts can help you navigate complex cultural dynamics and avoid common pitfalls.

Clarify Expectations

To mitigate misunderstandings, clearly articulate goals, timelines, and next steps. Follow up with detailed documentation to ensure alignment.

Build Trust Over Time

Invest in long-term relationships rather than focusing solely on immediate gains. Trust is often the currency of cross-cultural negotiations and can unlock opportunities beyond the initial deal.

Cross-cultural negotiations require patience, empathy, and a willingness to adapt. By understanding and respecting cultural differences, negotiators can build stronger relationships, avoid misunderstandings, and achieve outcomes that benefit all parties. As history teaches us, whether you're trading spices or negotiating a global partnership, the key to success lies in finding common ground.

The Technology Factor

The world is in an unprecedented period of technological development and advancement. From generative AI, to 3D printing, to autonomous equipment and vehicles, these have all revolutionized how we work.[19] This is especially true in highly routinized tasks and activities. Here are some additional considerations.

Digital Tools—Because Excel Isn't Always the Answer

Gone are the days when negotiations were conducted solely with notepads and handshakes. Today, digital tools have revolutionized the negotiation process, enabling greater precision, efficiency, and collaboration. From contract management systems to market intelligence platforms, these tools turn data into actionable insights, ensuring negotiators have the tools they need at the table.

Modern Negotiation Tools

While the East India Company negotiated with sabers, today we take a different approach.

Contract Management Systems

Streamlining the creation, storage, and management of contracts, these systems ensure transparency, compliance, and traceability throughout the process.

The East India Company relied on meticulous handwritten contracts to maintain its trade monopoly. Today, platforms like DocuSign and Icertis automate workflows, track changes, and maintain version control.

Pricing Analytics

Dynamic pricing tools provide insights into market conditions, competitor pricing, and cost structures, enabling negotiators to make data-driven decisions.

Silk Road merchants tracked the fluctuating value of goods like silk, spices, and gold along different trade routes, adjusting their prices accordingly to maximize profits.

Market Intelligence Platforms

Comprehensive data on suppliers, buyers, and market conditions is invaluable for negotiation preparation. Platforms like Gartner, Bloomberg Terminal, and others aggregate data, providing actionable insights.

In the Roman Empire, scouts and diplomats gathered intelligence on trade opportunities and regional conditions to inform their negotiation strategies, particularly in securing critical resources like grain.

Communication Platforms

Effective communication is the backbone of any negotiation. Digital platforms like Zoom, Microsoft Teams, and Slack enable seamless collaboration, even across time zones.

Merchants on the Silk Road developed standardized trade languages and symbolic systems to facilitate communication across diverse cultures—a historical precursor to today's digital communication tools.

Documentation Management

Keeping track of negotiation documents, agreements, and correspondence is critical for maintaining accountability and ensuring alignment. Tools like Google Workspace, Dropbox, and SharePoint simplify document sharing and collaboration.

The meticulous recordkeeping of the East India Company ensured that agreements, correspondence, and financial transactions were preserved, enabling the organization to maintain control over its far-flung operations.

Digital tools have transformed negotiations, replacing guesswork with data and enabling collaboration across geographies and time zones. However, like any tool, their value depends on how effectively they're used. By integrating these platforms into the negotiation process, businesses can achieve greater transparency, efficiency, and success.

As history shows, whether you're trading spices or software licenses, the tools at your disposal can make all the difference.

Data Analytics—Numbers Don't Lie, but They Do Hide Sometimes

In the world of negotiations, data is both a compass and a magnifying glass. It guides decision-making and reveals hidden opportunities or risks that might otherwise go unnoticed. From analyzing price trends to benchmarking performance, data analytics empowers negotiators to back their decisions with facts rather than assumptions. Yet, like any powerful tool, it must be wielded wisely. Because while numbers don't lie, they can sometimes obscure the full picture.

Key Metrics

To better understand the different types of data, focus on these areas

Price Trend Analysis
Understanding historical and current price trends helps negotiators anticipate future movements and establish realistic benchmarks.

The global semiconductor shortage caused price volatility across the electronics industry. Companies that used price trend analysis to secure fixed-price agreements early in the crisis saved millions compared to those forced to buy at inflated market rates later.

Silk Road merchants tracked seasonal fluctuations in the demand for goods like spices and silk. For instance, silk prices often peaked during winter in Europe, allowing traders to maximize profits by timing their shipments strategically.

Performance Metrics

Evaluating supplier or buyer performance provides critical insights into reliability, quality, and efficiency, ensuring that negotiations are based on more than just price.

Think of a modern multinational retailer negotiating a $500 million logistics contract using performance metrics such as on-time delivery rates, damage claims, and potential partners, including delivery metrics.

The East India Company maintained detailed records of supplier performance, noting which ports delivered goods on time and which regions struggled with reliability. These insights informed future trade agreements.

Market Benchmarks

Comparing contract terms, pricing, and service levels against industry standards ensures that negotiators aren't overpaying or underselling.

In 2022, an energy company used market benchmarks to renegotiate a long-term fuel supply contract. By comparing their existing terms to current industry averages, they identified $30 million in potential savings over the contract's duration.[20]

Roman merchants benchmarked prices across Mediterranean ports, ensuring they didn't overpay for goods like grain or olive oil. These benchmarks helped maintain profitability and competitiveness.

Cost Modeling

Breaking down the TCO—including acquisition, maintenance, and disposal—provides a comprehensive view of a deal's true value.

A global automotive manufacturer negotiating a $1 billion parts supply agreement used cost modeling to evaluate long-term costs. This analysis revealed hidden expenses in transportation and storage, prompting renegotiation and saving $50 million over five years.

The East India Company calculated not only the purchase price of spices but also shipping, storage, and distribution costs to determine the profitability of each route. This holistic approach allowed the Company to have complete visibility into TCO of their goods.

Risk Assessment

Identifying and quantifying potential risks—such as supply disruptions, price volatility, or geopolitical instability—ensures negotiators can proactively address vulnerabilities.

During the COVID-19 pandemic, a pharmaceutical company used risk assessment models to evaluate potential supply chain disruptions. This analysis led to the diversification of suppliers, ensuring uninterrupted production and saving an estimated $200 million in lost revenue.[21]

Silk Road traders constantly assessed risks like bandit attacks, political instability, and natural disasters. Caravan leaders often adjusted routes or hired additional guards based on these assessments, minimizing losses and ensuring safe delivery of goods.

Strategies for Leveraging Data Analytics

You've heard the expression "garbage in, garbage out"? Well, this is especially true in data analytics. Focus on these strategies

1. **Centralize Data Sources:**
   Consolidate data from multiple platforms into a single dashboard to gain a comprehensive view of trends, performance, and risks.

2. **Invest in Predictive Analytics:**
   Use advanced tools to forecast market changes, anticipate challenges, and identify opportunities.

3. **Collaborate with Stakeholders:**
   Share insights with team members, suppliers, and partners to align goals and make data-driven decisions.

4. **Regularly Update Metrics:**
   Data is only as valuable as it is current. Regularly refresh datasets to ensure relevance and accuracy during negotiations.

5. **Train Teams in Data Interpretation:**
   Equip negotiators with the skills to analyze and interpret data effectively, ensuring they can translate insights into actionable strategies.

Data analytics is the foundation of informed negotiation strategies. By leveraging metrics like price trends, performance benchmarks, and risk assessments, negotiators can approach the table with confidence and clarity. As history shows, whether you're transporting silk across the desert or securing a multimillion-dollar contract, the ability to interpret and act on data can mean the difference between success and failure.

THE BOTTOM LINE:
LEVERAGE COMES FROM LISTENING

Modern value chain negotiation is an art form that would make our Roman friend's head spin. While we're not negotiating for live sharks anymore—usually—the principles remain the same: Understand your position, create value, build relationships, and always have a backup plan.

Remember: The best negotiations aren't about winning or losing; they're about creating sustainable value for all parties. Unless you're negotiating for sharks—then it's probably best to just pay what they're asking and hope everything arrives alive.

Because in the end, whether you're a Roman procuring exotic animals or a modern value chain manager sourcing avocados, the goal is the same: Get what you need at a price you can afford, when you want it, while keeping everyone happy enough to do business again tomorrow.

Some negotiations are better left to history.

CHAPTER 5

THE NEGOTIATION PLAYBOOK

Up until now, we've been discussing broad themes and concepts. This next topic provides both industry-agnostic steps and the context you need to master the art and science of negotiation.

Pre-Negotiation:
Do Your Homework or Don't Bother Showing Up

Negotiation is a game of strategy, preparation, and execution. Those who approach the table without a clear plan risk losing more than just favorable terms—they risk their credibility and long-term business viability. This playbook delves into the critical pre-negotiation steps that separate the amateurs from the experts, enriched with historical lessons and modern examples.

Research and Preparation

Preparation is everything. The most successful negotiators spend far more time researching and strategizing than they do at the table. As the East India Company demonstrated during its centuries-long reign over global trade, knowledge is power, and preparation is the key to unlocking it.[1]

But what exactly should you be researching?

Market Analysis

Understanding market dynamics is the cornerstone of effective negotiation. The East India Company excelled by tracking global demand for spices, textiles, and tea, while identifying regions where these goods commanded the highest premiums. For instance, they knew that Indian cotton could fetch up to three times its local price in European markets, shaping their trade routes and pricing strategies.[2]

In today's world, market analysis involves studying industry trends, competitive pricing, and economic forecasts. For example, when Tesla negotiates lithium contracts, it considers not only current market rates but also projections for EV adoption and government regulations on renewable energy.[3] The goal is to anticipate market movements and negotiate from a position of informed confidence.

Supplier/Buyer Research

Knowing the other party's strengths, weaknesses, and motivations provides a crucial edge. The East India Company often sent envoys to study local rulers' economic needs and political pressures, using this intelligence to craft mutually beneficial agreements.[4]

Modern negotiators can achieve similar insights through financial analysis, customer reviews, and even social media activity. For example, if a supplier is facing cash flow issues or excess inventory, you can leverage this information to secure better terms. Conversely, understanding a buyer's strategic goals can help you position your offer as essential to their success.

Alternative Options

Diversification was the East India Company's insurance policy against disruption. If piracy made one route unsafe, they pivoted to another. If a key supplier became unreliable, they had backups ready. This flexibility allowed the Company to maintain continuity in even the most volatile conditions.

Modern value chains demand the same level of preparedness. Companies that rely on a single supplier are always vulnerable to disruptions,[5] By cultivating multiple supplier relationships or identifying alternative sources, businesses gain leverage and reduce risk.

BATNA Development
(Best Alternative to a Negotiated Agreement)

The East India Company's fallback options often included naval enforcement, alternative markets, or temporary supply reductions to pressure the other party. While today's negotiations are less combative, a strong BATNA remains essential.

A BATNA provides leverage by ensuring you have a viable path forward if negotiations falter. For example, a retailer negotiating with a logistics provider might prepare a BATNA by identifying alternative carriers or exploring in-house delivery options.[6] This strengthens your position and reduces the risk of being forced into unfavorable terms.

Strategy Development

Preparation is incomplete without a robust strategy. Knowing what you want, what you can concede, and where you'll draw the line provides clarity and focus during negotiations. Pay particular attention to:

Objective Setting

Clear objectives ensure team alignment and focus. For the East India Company, objectives often included securing trade exclusivity, gaining access to key ports, or reducing tariffs. These goals were tied to broader strategic plans, such as dominating the spice trade or expanding textile exports.[7]

Modern objectives might include achieving cost reductions, securing supply chain resilience, or fostering innovation through collaboration. For example, when Walmart negotiates with suppliers, its objectives often include maintaining low prices while ensuring ethical sourcing practices—a delicate balance requiring strategic precision.[8]

Red Line Identification

Every negotiation has its limits. For the East India Company, red lines included territorial sovereignty and trade monopolies. When local rulers refused to comply, the Company often walked away—or escalated to more aggressive measures.

Today, red lines might include nonnegotiable quality standards, delivery timelines, or intellectual property protections. For example, pharmaceutical companies are unlikely to compromise on IP clauses, as these assets represent the core of their business. Defining these boundaries in advance ensures consistency and focus under pressure.[9]

Concession Planning

Effective negotiators understand that flexibility is key. The East India Company often offered concessions, such as reduced tariffs or military assistance, to secure lucrative agreements. These concessions were carefully calculated to maximize long-term gains.

Modern negotiators should approach concessions with the same level of precision. This might involve offering extended payment terms, cobranding opportunities, or shared infrastructure investments. For instance, Amazon frequently negotiates tax incentives with local governments in exchange for job creation and investment in regional infrastructure.[10]

Team Alignment

The East India Company's negotiation teams often included diplomats, traders, and military officers, each playing a specific role. This alignment ensured cohesive, strategic efforts.[11]

Team alignment is equally critical in modern negotiations. Before entering discussions, all team members must understand the objectives, strategy, and roles they will play. For example, a legal adviser might handle specific contract issues such as indemnity, while a procurement specialist focuses on schedule, cost, and quality considerations. A disjointed team signals weakness and can undermine even the strongest strategy.

Negotiation isn't simply about sitting at the table; it's about the groundwork you lay before you get there. By investing time in research, preparation, and strategy development, businesses can negotiate from a position of strength, ensuring outcomes that drive long-term value.

DURING NEGOTIATION: THE DANCE OF THE DEAL

Negotiation is a delicate dance where timing, strategy, and finesse all play a crucial role in determining the outcome. From the marketplaces of the Silk Road to the high-stakes boardrooms of today, this process has always involved opening moves, a tactical middle game, and a well-executed close. Each phase builds on the last, blending relationship building with value creation. Just like the East India Company's meticulous contracts or the cultural diplomacy of Silk Road merchants, success hinges on a balance of preparation, adaptability, and trust.

Opening Moves

The opening stage of any negotiation sets the tone for what follows. It's a high-stakes moment where first impressions matter and strategic positioning begins. Key factors include:

Anchor Setting

On the Silk Road, merchants often started negotiations with inflated opening prices, setting an anchor point from which to bargain.[12] This tactic remains relevant today. Whether you're negotiating supplier contracts or pricing agreements, setting the first number gives you control over the conversation's framework.

When the East India Company negotiated spice prices in Southeast Asia, it anchored its opening bids low, knowing local merchants would counter high. The resulting midpoint usually fell within the Company's target range. This tactic remains common at car dealerships—it's one of the oldest negotiation techniques.

Initial Proposals

The first offer is more than just a number; it's a statement of intent. Effective initial proposals are grounded in research and reflect both ambition and pragmatism.

During the Roman Empire's trade negotiations, emissaries proposed terms that included mutually beneficial trade routes, resource sharing, and military protection. These offers often appealed to both economic and political interests.[13]

Response Strategies

Just as you make an opening move, the other party will counter. Successful negotiators plan for various responses, adapting quickly to keep the conversation aligned with their objectives.

In 1615, when the East India Company faced higher-than-expected demands from Mughal Emperor Jahangir, its response involved offering British naval protection for Mughal ports—a concession that strengthened both sides.[14]

Relationship Building

The Silk Road on relationships, with merchants cultivating trust through gifts, hospitality, and shared stories.[15] We still do this today in modern negotiations. Building rapport at the outset fosters goodwill, and having a personal rapport with your counterpart often helps resolve conflicts before they escalate. When serious issues do pop up, a strong relationship can make resolution faster, easier, and less likely to derail the entire deal.

The Middle Game

The bulk of the negotiation is the give-and-take that determines value and resolves challenges. I call this "the Middle Game," and it's when both parties strive for:

Value Creation

Beyond haggling over price, successful negotiators focus on creating value for both sides. This might include offering additional services, bundling products, or solving a partner's pain points.

When the East India Company negotiated exclusive trade rights in Bengal, for example, it created value by offering advanced European textiles and naval protection in exchange for favorable trade terms.[16]

Problem-Solving

Negotiations rarely proceed without obstacles. Effective negotiators address problems collaboratively, turning potential deal-breakers into opportunities for innovation.

On the Silk Road, language barriers were a common challenge. Traders overcame this by developing pidgin languages or hiring interpreters, ensuring smooth transactions.[17]

Concession Management

Every negotiation involves compromise. The key is managing concessions strategically, giving ground on less important points to gain advantages on critical issues.

During the Roman Empire's negotiations with tribal leaders, the promise of citizenship or tax reductions often secured loyalty, even when territorial disputes persisted.[18]

Progress Tracking

Keeping track of agreements and unresolved issues ensures momentum and prevents misunderstandings. Modern tools like collaborative software mirror the detailed ledgers once maintained by Silk Road merchants to document trades and payments.[19]

Closing

This phase, the close, is where deals are sealed—or fall apart. Closing isn't only about reaching an agreement; it's about ensuring clarity and setting the stage for a strong partnership. It involves:

Agreement Confirmation

The East India Company's contracts often included ceremonies where agreements were publicly declared, reinforcing trust and mutual accountability.[20] Today, confirmation generally involves clear agreement followed by detailed documentation.

Documentation

Modern-day contracts, with scope, schedules, and appendices, protect both parties and clarify expectations. For example, Roman merchants frequently used clay tablets to record trade details, ensuring both parties had a tangible reference.[21]

Planning Next Steps

Closing may be the end of the negotiation, but it's just the beginning of the execution. Defining next steps ensures smooth implementation while preventing delays.

When Amazon negotiates major contracts with logistics providers, for example, the closing phase includes detailed action plans outlining delivery schedules, performance metrics, and escalation processes.[22]

Relationship Reinforcement

The end of negotiation is the perfect time to strengthen relationships. Expressing gratitude, reaffirming commitments, and demonstrating goodwill all build trust for the future.

Post-Agreement Contract Management

A deal is only as good as its execution. Managing the contract over its life cycle is critical to maintaining value and addressing challenges. This part of contract negotiation is often the least understood. Ask yourself: Who will administer the contract, enforce provisions, escalate issues, and pursue claim actions?

The contract must be very accessible and usable for the end user. Fancy legal jargon and circular references render the contract virtually useless when your teams actually need to resolve an issue. For that reason, be sure your contracts cover what to do in these situations:

Scope Creep: How will changes to the original deliverables be handled and approved?

Performance Issues: What mechanisms exist if the supplier underperforms—penalties, service credits, or re-procurement rights?

Disputes: How will disagreements—whether financial, operational, or legal—be identified, escalated, and resolved?

Reporting and Compliance: What reporting requirements exist for spend, KPIs, ESG metrics, or regulatory frameworks, and how will compliance with obligations like Supplier Codes of Conduct (SCOCs) be monitored?

Force Majeure and Disruption: What happens if external events—geopolitical, environmental, or logistical—prevent one party from meeting obligations?

Termination and Renewal: Who makes the call and under what conditions? What support is required?

Post-agreement management is where governance meets operations. It's the daily discipline of making sure the ink on the page translates into real performance, value, and accountability across the value chain.

THE BOTTOM LINE: DEALS DON'T END AT SIGNATURE

Negotiation is not a onetime event—it's a recurring play in the value chain game. The strongest negotiators understand that every deal is both an ending and a beginning, shaping the trust, credibility, and alliances that carry forward into the next round. Whether you're bargaining over procurement contracts, board-room decisions, or global partnerships, the same principles apply: Prepare with discipline, create clarity, and aim for outcomes that strengthen—not weaken—the chain.

Because in the end, the best negotiators don't just "win" deals. They build durable relationships, set the tone for future coopera-tion, and ensure the organization has the leverage and resilience to succeed in whatever ancient or modern arena it's competing in. That's not just good negotiation—it's good business.

CHAPTER 6

PARTNERSHIPS
AND ALLIANCES

If the East India Company had a Tinder profile, its relationship status would have been "It's Complicated." Swipe right and you'd find a global trading empire built not only on ships and spices but on a tangled web of strategic alliances, puppet partnerships, and questionable ethics, all dressed up as mutually beneficial trade.

But before colonial tea parties turned into boardroom takeovers, ancient empires had already mastered the fine art of collaboration. The Roman Empire didn't conquer the known world on its own; it absorbed local rulers into its structure, making them honorary Romans—with less honor, more taxes.[1] And the Silk Road? It wasn't a solo expedition; it was a series of handoffs, a global relay race of trust, trade, and terra-cotta.[2]

From supply routes guarded by Persian tribes to partnerships between Venetian merchants and Ottoman middlemen, the backbone of every major value chain has always been the same: alliances. Sometimes formal, sometimes fragile, often messy—but always absolutely necessary.

Today, little has changed. Your supply chain isn't a straight line, it's a dance floor. And whether you're waltzing with warehouse operators, tangoing with third-party logistics firms, or cha-cha-ing through procurement consortia, the success of your value chain hinges on your ability to partner well and partner wisely.

This chapter explores why partnerships matter, how to structure them to avoid disaster, and where things can go sideways faster than a Roman chariot in rush hour. We'll weave in examples old and new, show you what good governance looks like when no one wants to own the problem, and equip you with the tools to ensure your alliances aren't merely ceremonial scrolls but durable, scalable engines of shared value.

And yes, there will be sharks. Eventually.

THE HISTORICAL BLUEPRINT
OF PARTNERSHIPS

Spoiler alert: Trust is what you write in the preamble. Leverage is what shows up in the clauses.

Long before shareholder agreements and nondisclosure clauses, alliances were struck with blood, wine, or whatever local currency of loyalty was on hand. But make no mistake, value chains have always relied on partnerships. The trick wasn't just forming them; the trick was surviving them. Throughout history, the most successful value chains didn't only rely on logistics, supply, or even strategy—they relied on partnerships. Some were elegant, others exploitative, but all were essential. From emperors to merchants to monarchs, the leaders who built empires understood one thing:

You can't scale alone. You need others, and ideally, you need them to think they need you more than you need them.

Here are the three foundational partnership models that shaped global trade long before spreadsheets, ERPs, and joint venture boards.

Rome's Empire of Embedded Partnerships

The Romans were master collaborators. Instead of managing every outpost directly, they co-opted local rulers, governors, and even rival warlords into Roman administration. Think of it as an early franchise model, only with fewer branding guidelines and more crucifixions.

These arrangements were brilliant in theory: The locals focused on maintaining order, collecting taxes, and sending grain and gladiators to Rome. In return, they got roads, Roman citizenship—eventually—and the pleasure of not being sacked. Sound familiar? Herod the Great is a classic example: He ruled Judea under Roman authority. He got autonomy to build monuments, including a small renovation you may have heard of—the Second Temple—while Rome got access to Judea's resources and a compliant local figurehead.[3]

Think of today's multinational corporations entering emerging markets. They grant regional distributors "exclusive" rights to sell, market, and sometimes even co-brand the product—a modern nod to Roman client kinship. But behind the scenes? Headquarters still holds the veto power. Pricing? Must align with global strategy. Branding? Locked down tighter than a Vatican archive. Territory expansion? Only with corporate blessing and after twelve rounds of regional VP sign-off.

This model creates the illusion of local autonomy while preserving centralized control. It's thinly veiled imperialism with a performance dashboard. Your local partner gets enough room to operate—but just not enough rope to change the narrative. Any deviation from the script, and the distributor finds themselves suddenly "off strategy," replaced by a new partner who happens to speak Latin—or at least corporate English.

And yet these partnerships persist because they provide local access, labor flexibility, and political insulation. The trick—just like in Rome—is keeping the locals empowered enough to perform but never independent enough to defect.

Today's empires come with brand guidelines and CRM systems, but the governance structure often mirrors ancient Rome more than we'd like to admit.

Rome's greatest strength, its ability to partner with and absorb local leadership, was also its most persistent blind spot. When those relationships were misaligned or abused, the entire value chain fractured. Supplies dried up, borders destabilized, and communication collapsed. Rebellion wasn't always about independence; sometimes it was about broken agreements, ignored needs, or heavy-handed governors who forgot they were partners, not overlords.

Modern governance models face the same trap. It's easy to set up the *appearance* of structure: approval matrices, shared dashboards, escalation protocols. But if partners aren't truly aligned in vision, incentives, and authority, these tools become performative.

Caesar didn't lose control because he lacked power—he lost it because the grain shipments stopped arriving.

The real failure point? Rome mistook silence for loyalty and delegation for trust. Food riots in Rome weren't always about empty stomachs—they were about injustice, neglect, and leaders who ignored local needs. When grain ran short, armies faltered, cities rioted, and allies disappeared.

Governance without alignment isn't a safeguard, it's a blind spot. Without shared goals, constant communication, and actual accountability, even the most structured partnerships will collapse under the weight of unspoken expectations.

The Silk Road: Trade by Trust and Terra-Cotta

The Silk Road, the world's original LinkedIn, wasn't controlled by any one empire or corporation. It was a patchwork of partnerships: Chinese producers, central Asian middlemen, Persian brokers, and Roman consumers—who never quite grasped where silk came from but *really* liked it.

Every link in the chain relied on informal partnerships and mutual interest. Goods changed hands dozens of times, and trust had to be reestablished at every *caravanserai*. It was less end-to-end visibility and more "I sure hope the guy three stops back isn't the one following me."

Still, this system endured for centuries. Why? Because each partner, no matter how small, knew their role, understood their risk, and had just enough incentive not to torch the entire network.

If Rome was about centralized control, the Silk Road was about decentralized trust. There was no empire overseeing the four-thousand-mile network from China to the Mediterranean. No customs office. No shared ERP. Just an informal agreement: Don't steal, don't swindle (too much), and try not to die.

The Silk Road wasn't a road so much as a relay—a baton pass of silk, spices, ideas, and sometimes a plague or two. No single merchant made the full journey. Goods would change hands, languages, currencies, and sometimes camel species at each stop. What held it together? A mix of reputation, ritual, risk mitigation, a lot of handwritten IOUs, and some serious cultural improvisation.

Caravanserais—*The Original Cross-Dock*

Every twenty to thirty miles along the route sat a *caravanserai*, part truck stop, part trade hub, part rumor mill. Here, goods were inspected, deals were brokered, and news was exchanged: which passes were snowed in, which tribe was charging too much for "protection," and who had defaulted on their salt loan in Samarkand.[4]

It was also where informal partnerships were born. A Chinese silk merchant might partner with a Persian trader for the next leg, who then passed cargo to an Armenian middleman, who sold it to a Roman importer. No NDAs, no scorecards, just a shared interest in getting paid and staying alive.

Profit margins were based on risk, not volume.[5] The more dangerous the segment, the more expensive your markup. Today we call this dynamic pricing.

Modern Parallel—Tier-2 and Tier-3 Transparency

Today's global supply chains are more like the Silk Road than we care to admit. You may know your direct supplier. Maybe even your supplier's supplier. But do you know where your cobalt is mined? Who actually processes your packaging resin? Or who delivers the final unit to that last-mile customer in Kuala Lumpur?

Most companies don't. Like the Silk Road, modern supply chains run on partial visibility, relational trust, and a whole lot of assumed compliance. And just like the caravan traders of old, many rely on word-of-mouth vetting, past performance, and the vague hope that everyone down the line is behaving.

This model works…until it doesn't. When one link in the chain breaks—a flood, a factory fire, a civil war, or a pandemic—the whole system grinds to a halt. Just like the Silk Road collapsed when geopolitical tensions made certain trade routes impassable, adding on plague outbreaks compounded the disruption.

What the Silk Road Got Right:

Redundancy: Multiple overlapping routes gave traders options when one path was blocked—a principle modern companies forget until you have a blocked canal or a port strike.

Localized Intelligence: Partnerships at each node meant real-time updates from people on the ground. Today's equivalent is less camel scout, more emails from customs brokers, but the need is the same.

Relational Contracts: Agreements were enforced by reputation, not regulation. Break trust in Kashgar, and word would travel faster than your spices.

Governance Insight

The Silk Road endured because each node had localized control paired with shared incentive. It was fragile, yes, but it was also resilient because no one entity controlled it all. And when something broke, the rest adapted.

That's the governance lesson: Not all partnerships need to be micromanaged; however, they all need to be maintained. Visibility, communication, and shared risk management are what made the Silk Road endure for centuries. Remove any one of those and you're just a lone trader in the desert—with a very expensive load of silk and no one to pass it to.

Colonial Europe: Partnerships with a Side of Piracy

Fast-forward to the age of empires, and you'll find the East India Company pioneering a new kind of alliance: the contractual monopoly. They forged partnerships with local rulers and merchants across India, China, and Southeast Asia—but often only after showing off their cannons.[6]

These "agreements" were often lopsided, but they created expansive, multi-continent value chains. The lesson here? Even imperial bullies needed intermediaries for local access, political cover, and plausible deniability. But when the partnerships crumbled, so did the empire. That's not just history. That's governance failure with powdered wigs.

In Bengal, the Company allied with Mir Jafar to overthrow the ruling Nawab. In return, it received favorable tax treatment, access to ports, and a clear path to consolidate power—a partnership forged in back rooms and battlefields. Elsewhere, it struck deals with Dutch traders, Mughal administrators, and anyone who could move cargo or curry favor.[7]

But the terms were rarely equitable. The Company wrote the contracts, enforced the rules, and changed the pricing when it suited them. It wasn't so much a partnership as a corporate-led compliance program, one where dissent was met with economic sanctions or, occasionally, an armed "escalation."

These partnerships collapsed because the imbalance proved unsustainable. The Company prioritized control over collaboration, and once local partners lost faith in the deal, rebellion followed. Sound familiar?

You'll recognize this model in modern partnerships where one party provides capital, IP, and oversight, and the other provides labor, local knowledge, and all the risk. These aren't partnerships. They're compliance frameworks with nicer logos.

In tech, this might look like a multinational outsourcing development to an offshore team with strict SLAs and zero say in road map decisions. In manufacturing, it's a "joint venture" where one partner funds everything and the other supplies a factory and political cover but no voting rights.

These arrangements may work in the short term, but over time, imbalance breeds disengagement. And disengagement leads to delivery issues, quiet exits, or public blowups that sound a lot like "We're reevaluating our vendor relationships."

The Company was also a case study in internal corruption. With limited oversight from London and enormous local power, Company agents often made side deals, diverted funds, and manipulated supply contracts for personal gain. It was a shadow economy inside a shadow empire—the kind modern companies now try to root out through compliance audits and whistleblower hotlines.[8]

Lessons from the Ledger Books of Empires

History provides lessons and insights that are relevant today; they are:

- Asymmetrical partnerships create instability over time. When power, control, and financial gain are concentrated with one party, the imbalance erodes trust and limits collaboration, ultimately weakening long-term operational performance.

- Local alignment is a critical component of execution risk management. Sustainable partnerships require that objectives are not only understood but owned by regional stakeholders with authority and incentive to deliver.

- Governance structures must evolve as partnerships scale. Initial frameworks may provide clarity, but without regular recalibration, they become outdated, unable to support the complexity, pace, or risk profile of maturing operations.

- Partnerships require shared incentives to maintain performance and engagement. If one party bears disproportionate responsibility without proportional benefit, motivation and accountability decline, often systemically and silently.

- Insufficient oversight creates exposure to internal fraud and operational leakage. In low-transparency environments, informal systems and unauthorized practices can develop beneath formal structures, increasing both financial and reputational risk.

- Dominance-based models limit agility in times of disruption. Partnerships built on control rather than collaboration often lack the resiliency needed to navigate changing geopolitical, regulatory, or economic conditions.

Relationships are hard. It doesn't matter whether they're personal or business relationships; all parties have roles, responsibilities, and goals.

Modern Alliances

If the Roman Empire, the Silk Road, and the East India Company taught us anything, it's that partnerships come in many forms—and that form matters. The structure of an alliance often dictates its success, especially under pressure. Whether you're sharing IP, splitting costs, or jointly managing a vendor relationship, the type of partnership you choose shapes your governance model, financial exposure, and strategic flexibility.

Below are the most common alliance structures in today's value chains—each with distinct benefits, risks, and use cases:

Joint Ventures (JVs)

Definition: A formal, co-owned entity created by two or more parties to pursue a shared business objective.

Use Case: Large-scale infrastructure projects, market expansion into new geographies, or codevelopment of products where both parties bring significant assets or IP.

Strategic Considerations:

- Require clear governance and an exit strategy

- Shared control can lead to misalignment without strong escalation mechanisms

- Often subject to complex regulatory and tax implications

JVs work best when each party has comparable leverage, defined roles, and aligned long-term goals. Without this, they risk an operational tug-of-war with no clear owner.

Strategic Supplier Relationships

Definition: Long-term commercial arrangements with key vendors that go beyond transactional purchasing.

Use Case: Single-source or high-volume suppliers where continuity, innovation, and cost control are critical.

Strategic Considerations:

- Should include performance-based incentives and regular reviews

- Joint business planning strengthens alignment and reduces friction

- Risks arise when performance issues go unaddressed or governance is too informal

These alliances function like the Roman model: local execution with central oversight. When managed well, they extend capability. When neglected, they become bottlenecks.

Licensing and Technology Partnerships

Definition: Agreements allowing one party to use another's intellectual property, technology, or brand assets.

Use Case: Market entry, product development, or leveraging existing R&D without duplicating investment.

Strategic Considerations:

- Must include protections around IP use, misuse, and enforcement

- Success depends on ongoing communication and alignment on brand standards or technical road maps

- Risk increases if dependencies are not mapped or mitigated

These partnerships are lean by design but vulnerable to misalignment and scope creep if governance is light or poorly defined.

Public-Private Partnerships

Definition: Collaborations between government entities and private companies to deliver infrastructure or public services.[9]

Use Case: Transportation, utilities, health care infrastructure, or ESG-related initiatives.

Strategic Considerations:

- High visibility, high scrutiny—governance must be transparent and auditable

- Often involve long-term risk sharing and the need for political navigation

- Require balance between public accountability and commercial viability

Like the East India Company, these partnerships operate at the intersection of policy and commerce—and must be designed to serve both masters.

Informal or Relationship-Based Alliances

Definition: Unstructured or lightly formalized partnerships based on mutual benefit, trust, and ongoing collaboration.

Use Case: Early-stage ventures, industry networks, or regionally complex markets where flexibility is key.

Strategic Considerations:

- Low governance overhead but high dependency on interpersonal trust

- Difficult to scale or replicate consistently

- Limited protection in the event of dispute or nonperformance

These are the modern Silk Roads—flexible, efficient, and resilient when managed carefully. But one missing link or misstep can destabilize the entire chain.

Choosing the Right Structure

No single model fits every situation. The right alliance structure depends on factors such as:

- Degree of control required

- Level of financial investment

- Duration and complexity of engagement

- Risk profile and regulatory environment

- Strategic importance to the core business

Choosing incorrectly, or applying the right structure without the right governance, can turn a strategic partnership into a strategic liability.

Strategic alliances are the value chain equivalent of a long-term commitment. These aren't casual flings; they're deep, integrated relationships where both parties invest significant resources and share long-term objectives. They require commitment, shared objectives, deep resource integration, joint innovation efforts, and shared risks and rewards.

Actionable Themes—Fraud, Finance, Governance, and Risk

Every partnership—regardless of its structure—carries embedded risk. The moment two organizations agree to share responsibilities, assets, or deliverables, the value chain becomes more exposed. While collaboration enables scale and capability, it also requires a deliberate focus on the four cornerstones of sustainable partnership management: fraud, finance, governance, and risk. Neglecting even one of these dimensions can quietly undermine performance or very publicly derail the relationship.

Fraud

Partnerships often create operational complexity, and with complexity comes opportunity—both legitimate *and* illicit. Fraud in alliance environments tends to manifest not through overt theft but through manipulated data, inflated invoicing, opaque subcontracting, or side agreements that escape scrutiny. These issues are exacerbated when responsibilities are fragmented across entities, and when neither party feels fully accountable for oversight.

The absence of direct control over a partner's internal systems, financial processes, or vendor relationships can result in blind spots. This makes it essential to embed financial transparency and auditability into the architecture of the partnership from day one. Clauses that enable open-book accounting, real-time reporting, and independent verification are not of mistrust but rather a sign of maturity.

The message is clear: In cross-organizational collaboration, governance must extend beyond your own walls. Internal compliance frameworks must be mirrored externally. Otherwise, the system becomes vulnerable to manipulation—sometimes from within.

Finance

Financial misalignment is one of the most consistent causes of partnership underperformance. While the strategic rationale for an alliance may be clear, the underlying financial structure must support mutual benefit, not just mutual dependence. Too often, one party bears most of the operational risk or capital investment, while the other benefits from preferred pricing, IP access, or distribution rights, with little accountability for outcomes.

To avoid this imbalance, partnerships must be underpinned by clear commercial logic, transparent cost structures, and adaptable models that reflect changing conditions. This means moving beyond static revenue-sharing agreements or rigid payment terms toward performance-based incentives, phased investment models, and shared cost-savings mechanisms.

Just as important is the discipline of financial monitoring. Revenue leakage, cost overruns, or unanticipated margin erosion are common in long-term alliances where financial reviews become infrequent or symbolic. Effective partnerships require financial stewardship from both sides and a shared understanding of value creation—not merely cost control.

Governance

Strong governance is the difference between a functioning partnership and an ongoing negotiation. It provides the scaffolding for decision-making, escalation, performance management, and accountability—without needlessly constraining execution. When alliances fail, it's often not due to lack of intent but because responsibilities were poorly defined, expectations weren't managed, and accountability wasn't enforced.

Governance in a partnership must be jointly designed and jointly maintained. This includes defining who owns what—strategically and operationally—how decisions are made, and what mechanisms exist for resolving disputes. Governance should also reflect the cadence and complexity of the engagement. A strategic supplier relationship may require quarterly business reviews and joint scorecards, while a coinvested JV may require a full board structure with delegated authority frameworks.

The most effective partnerships embed governance into the day-to-day, not simply the contract. When escalation protocols, success metrics, and issue management are institutionalized—not improvised—the relationship can remain productive even under stress.

Risk

Risk is the dimension most often deferred in alliance design—and most regretted once disruption occurs. Whether it's geopolitical instability, reputational fallout, regulatory misalignment, or operational dependency, risk in partnerships is rarely symmetrical. One partner may absorb more of the reputational fallout, while the other bears more financial exposure. Unless these realities are acknowledged and actively managed, partners may find themselves unprepared or unwilling to fully respond when things go wrong.

Effective partnerships incorporate joint risk planning as part of their foundational structure. This includes identifying critical points of dependency, mapping regional exposure, and developing shared continuity and contingency plans. Contracts should articulate not only the intent to collaborate but also the practical mechanisms for managing disruption—from force majeure to operational redundancy.

Perhaps most critically, risk should be managed as a living dimension of the partnership. As external conditions evolve, whether from climate events, market volatility, or shifting regulatory standards, the risk posture must be revisited, rescored, and rebalanced between parties.

In high-functioning alliances, these four pillars aren't afterthoughts, they're central to performance, trust, and resilience. Fraud prevention is built into the design. Financial models evolve with the relationship. Governance is not ceremonial but operational. And risk is shared not only in principle but in planning and response as well.

WHAT WORKS—AND WHAT DOESN'T

The success or failure of a partnership often has little to do with original intent and everything to do with structure and follow-through. Even the most compelling business case for collaboration can falter if roles are ambiguous, trust is unevenly distributed, or governance is treated as an afterthought. History, once again, offers plenty of precedent, as do modern business failures.

The Roman Empire's provincial model prospered when local governors were integrated into a cohesive administrative system with clear responsibilities and mutual benefit. It failed when these relationships became imbalanced, when regional leaders acted autonomously, communication broke down, and Rome's centralized authority no longer carried weight in practice.[10] The same risks exist today when large organizations operate with decentralized partnerships but lack the governance discipline to align and maintain them.

In contrast, the Silk Road offers a different lesson: Success in highly distributed, loosely structured systems depends on continuous information flow, mutual reliability, and trust-based incentives. It lacked a formal owner but endured for centuries because it was designed around interdependence rather than dominance. Each trader, handler, and broker understood their role in the broader system. No one could afford to disrupt the flow—not if they wanted to remain in business.

Modern alliances reflect both of these archetypes. Consider large technology companies partnering with start-ups in innovation ecosystems. These relationships often begin with shared ambition but fail due to unclear IP boundaries, misaligned commercial expectations, or the larger partner defaulting to a risk-averse legal position that stalls agility. On the other hand, public-private partnerships have demonstrated long-term resilience when contracts are supported by active joint governance, well-defined risk allocation, and periodic recalibration tied to performance reviews.

Across industries and models, certain partnership dynamics tend to repeat—either reinforcing success or accelerating breakdown.

What Works

Defined Accountability and Role Clarity:
Every partner must know their exact responsibilities, decision rights, and deliverables. The best-performing alliances codify this not only in contracts but also in day-to-day operations, ensuring clarity across teams, time zones, and leadership levels.

Aligned Incentives and Risk Sharing:
Partnerships that succeed financially are those in which rewards and risks are proportionate. If one party carries the investment while the other captures the upside, disengagement is a matter of when, not if. A codeveloped agreement where both parties invest resources and co-own the IP, for example, is far more stable.

Operational Cadence and Communication:
A structured rhythm of communication, performance review, and joint planning ensures alignment stays current. Whether it's quarterly steering committees, shared KPIs, or real-time dashboards, the ability to detect and resolve drift early is a hallmark of resilient partnerships.

Governance as Infrastructure:
Governance isn't simply documentation; it's the structure that supports decision-making, conflict resolution, and performance management. When done well, it creates consistency and predictability without stifling innovation or local adaptation.

Cultural Compatibility and Leadership Alignment:
Partnerships are ultimately executed by people. Shared values, compatible working styles, and mutual respect among leadership teams contribute just as much to long-term viability as legal structures and financial terms.

What Doesn't

In contrast, certain patterns consistently show up in failed partnerships—often gradually, then suddenly

- **Over-Indexing on the Contract, Under-Indexing on the Relationship:**
  While legal agreements are essential, they are not substitutes for trust, communication, and mutual engagement. A rigid contract without a working relationship is like a well-written user manual for a broken device—technically correct but practically useless.

- **Unbalanced Power Dynamics:**
  Alliances that lean too heavily in one partner's favor may function in stable environments but often crack under stress. The East India Company's relationships with local rulers operated on this imbalance efficiently in the short term, but ultimately they became unsustainable due to eroded autonomy and local resentment.

- **Inflexible Structures in Dynamic Markets:**
  Fixed-term pricing, static scopes of work, or narrowly
  defined success metrics can backfire in volatile environments. Partnerships that don't allow for reprioritization
  or recalibration in response to market shifts quickly lose
  strategic relevance.

- **Unmanaged Interdependence:**
  The more interconnected the workstreams, the greater
  the potential for cascading failure. Without clearly defined
  service levels, response protocols, or escalation channels,
  small issues in one partner's domain can quickly compromise the entire value chain.

- **Lack of Exit Strategy or Renewal Planning:**
  Partnerships rarely end when they should; they either fade
  into nonperformance or collapse under unresolved friction. Effective alliances have structured off-ramps, renewal
  criteria, and renegotiation triggers built in from the outset
  to allow graceful exits when needed.

From ancient trade routes to modern corporations, partnerships have been the backbone of successful value chains. Whether
it was Roman governors administering provinces on Caesar's
behalf, Silk Road merchants negotiating safe passage through
unfamiliar territories, or contemporary organizations aligning to
tackle climate goals and regulatory shifts, the partnerships that
endure are built on these timeless principles.

THE BOTTOM LINE:
DURABLE, NOT DECORATIVE

Partnerships are easy to declare and difficult to sustain. They look
good in press releases, strategic plans, and investor decks. In

practice they demand an ongoing investment of time, trust, and disciplined execution. When treated as symbolic gestures or short-term conveniences, partnerships unravel. When designed and governed with purpose, they become long-term strategic assets.

History is unambiguous on this point. Rome's empire expanded not through brute force alone but through systems of alliance that extended its influence across borders and cultures. The Silk Road endured because mutual benefit and communication were baked into its very existence. And the East India Company, while powerful, ultimately lost control when its partnerships turned into exploitative arrangements devoid of trust or balance.

In today's complex and interdependent world, the stakes are even higher. Global challenges—from geopolitical volatility to climate transition—require new forms of collaboration that are both resilient and responsive. No single organization can solve these problems alone, nor should they try. But alliances forged without structure, alignment, and mutual value will not withstand pressure, regardless of intent.

To build durable partnerships, individuals must move beyond handshakes and headline statements. They must operationalize trust through governance. They must protect alignment through structured communication. And they must treat value creation as an active, evolving commitment, not a onetime deal.

A partnership is not a shortcut. It's not a workaround. It's a deliberate strategy to extend capability and create shared outcomes, and it should be approached with the same rigor, accountability, and foresight as any other enterprise investment.

Durability isn't an accident. It's a choice—one made not at the signing of the agreement but in every decision, meeting, and conflict that follows.

CHAPTER 7

INFLATION AND
ECONOMIC PRESSURES

Want to know how Roman emperors dealt with inflation? When the empire's treasuries ran dry, their solution was as simple as it was disastrous: They diluted the silver content in their coins and hoped no one noticed.[1]

Unsurprisingly, people did notice. By the time Diocletian (284–305 CE) tried to fix the mess with price controls and economic reforms, the damage was irreversible. The Roman currency had lost much of its value, merchants demanded payments in foreign coins, and the economy struggled under the weight of mistrust and inefficiency.[2]

Fast-forward to today, and while we may not be mixing copper into silver coins, inflation continues to wreak havoc on global economies and supply chains. The mechanisms have grown more sophisticated: Central banks tweak interest rates, governments print money, and markets respond. But the underlying challenge remains: How do you manage a value chain when the cost of everything keeps rising, often unpredictably?

THE MONEY GAMES

As you are acutely aware, inflation isn't merely an abstract financial concept. It's a living, breathing problem that eats away at margins, destabilizes operations, and forces tough decisions. In a world where costs for raw materials, labor, energy, and transportation are skyrocketing, managing a stable supply chain can feel like trying to hold water in a sieve.

Why Everything Costs More

Inflation's impact ripples across every aspect of the value chain, creating a perfect storm of rising costs and logistical complexity. Its roots are multifaceted, drawing from historical precedents and modern economic pressures alike.

Take raw materials, for example. In ancient Rome, grain was the lifeblood of the empire, and its price fluctuations could spark riots. When Julius Caesar imported massive quantities of grain in 58 BCE to feed Rome's growing population, the sudden demand caused prices to spike by as much as 30 percent, creating unrest among the city's poorest citizens.[3]

Today, the stakes are no less dire. Between 2020 and 2023, the price of steel swung wildly, surging over 300 percent at one point, disrupting industries from construction to automotive manufacturing. Such volatility forces modern companies to rethink their sourcing strategies, balancing cost with availability to stabilize—or sometimes destabilize—entire value chains.

Labor costs have always been a persistent challenge. In Rome, plagues such as the Antonine Plague (165–180 CE) devastated the workforce, killing an estimated 10 percent of the population. The consequences were far-reaching: Wages soared, food shortages became frequent, and landowners were forced to adapt. Some turned to labor-saving tools, while others reverted to forced labor—an approach that ultimately deepened political and social instability.[4]

Modern parallels abound. In the post-COVID era, in 2022, global labor costs rose sharply, with wages in the US increasing by 5.6 percent, the fastest rate increase in decades. For industries like logistics and manufacturing, already squeezed by razor-thin margins, this escalation required creative solutions such as automation or offshore production—both of which brought their own risks and complexities.

Energy prices add another layer of uncertainty. The Romans may not have worried about oil prices, but their economy depended heavily on energy-intensive resources like wood and charcoal. By the first century CE, deforestation in provinces like Britain forced them to seek alternative building materials, increasing costs and slowing construction projects.[5] Fast-forward to 2022, when geopolitical tensions drove oil prices to record highs, impacting everything from transportation to factory operations. For modern value chains, energy price volatility is a critical factor to consider.

Transportation costs, a cornerstone of supply chain logistics, are no less susceptible to inflation. In ancient Rome, a single storm could devastate the grain supply, as happened in 62 CE, when a fleet was destroyed en route to the capital, causing grain prices to triple in some regions.[6] Today, disruptions like the 2021 *Ever Given* blockage in the Suez Canal can send container shipping rates soaring by over 400 percent in a matter of weeks. For businesses, these sudden surges demand agile contingency planning and diversified logistics strategies to maintain operational continuity.

Learning From History

Inflation, as history shows, is not only about rising prices; it's about trust, adaptability, and innovation. The Romans lost trust in their currency when emperors debased coins, leading to a breakdown in economic systems—launching the decline of the Roman Empire.

For modern businesses, transparency and strong supplier relationships are critical to maintaining stability during inflationary periods.

Innovation is another essential lesson. When faced with labor shortages or resource scarcities, Roman engineers didn't just lament their fate—they built infrastructure and pioneered new construction techniques to maximize resource efficiency. Modern practitioners must adopt a similar mindset, embracing technologies like automation, AI, and predictive analytics to offset rising costs and build resilient value chains.

Finally, adaptability remains key. The Romans learned the hard way that rigid systems cannot withstand the pressures of a changing economy. Today's businesses must build flexibility into their value chains, diversifying suppliers, sourcing locally when feasible, and creating contingency plans for transportation and production disruptions.

Navigating Inflation Today

Modern inflation challenges demand a combination of historical wisdom and modern ingenuity. From Julius Caesar's grain imports to the *Ever Given*'s impact on shipping rates, the lessons are clear: Inflation is as much about strategy as it is about economics. Think of it as a test of leadership, creativity, and resilience.

For today's value chain teams, success means embracing the unexpected, planning for volatility, and—most importantly—learning from the past.

FOUR DRIVERS OF ECONOMIC PRESSURE

In the battle for value chain resilience, inflation isn't the only adversary. Enter the Four Drivers of Economic Pressure: cost inflation, supply chain disruption, demand volatility, and currency risk. These challenges can dismantle even the most carefully crafted value chain strategies, forcing businesses to adapt—or perish.

Driver #1:
Cost Inflation

Cost inflation silently erodes profitability. Unlike sudden shocks, inflation creeps in, gradually tightening margins across sourcing, manufacturing, logistics, and labor. For many organizations, the impact isn't noticed until profits disappear.

Ancient Rome grappled with similar inflationary pressures. Grain, a staple import from Egypt, was the lifeblood of the empire's food supply. When poor harvests or political unrest disrupted the grain trade, prices surged. To prevent civil instability, emperors instituted rationing systems and price controls—tools still recognizable even in today's economic playbook.[7]

Fast-forward to the present, where inflationary pressures are more complex, more global. Between 2021 and 2023, steel prices tripled, energy markets spiked, and transportation costs surged due to fuel volatility and labor shortages. For industries dependent on predictable input costs, from construction to automotive, this was not merely a margin squeeze—it became a significant disruption.

Modern value chain practitioners are responding with layered strategies. Contract renegotiation has become a tactical necessity, while nearshoring and local sourcing are now key components of cost containment and risk mitigation. Automation and digital procurement tools help companies manage rising labor costs and streamline operations.

Takeaway: Cost inflation cannot be eliminated, but it can be absorbed, through operational flexibility, disciplined procurement, and strategic cost control. Those who treat inflation as a permanent variable rather than a temporary anomaly will outperform in the long term.

Cost Inflation

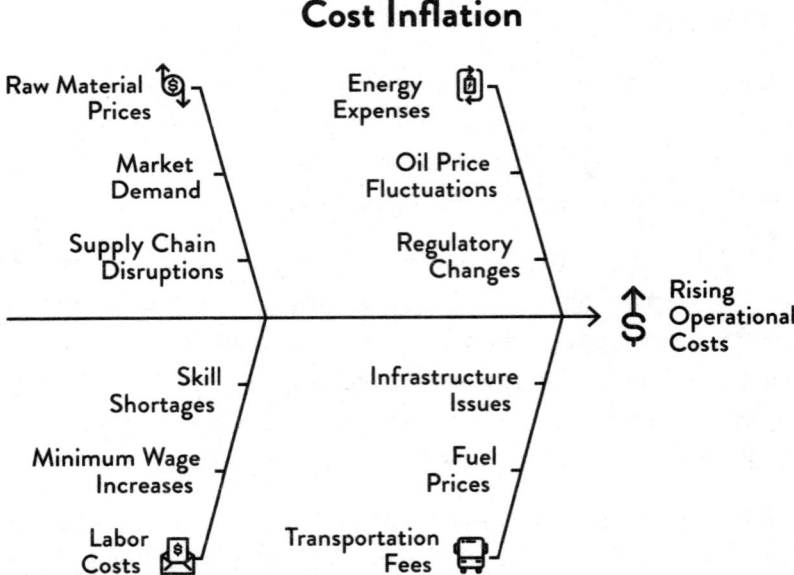

Driver #2:
Supply Chain Disruption

Disruption has replaced efficiency as the dominant narrative in supply chain management. For decades, the prevailing model optimized for cost and speed. But recent events—from COVID-19 to geopolitical instability—show that resilience now trumps optimization.[8]

Today's leaders must design for disruption. That means diversifying suppliers across regions, building buffer inventory where justified, investing in real-time visibility, and reassessing just-in-time models. Digital twins, predictive analytics, and supply chain risk modeling are becoming core capabilities rather than distant aspirations.

Takeaway: Resilience is not redundancy, it's strategic optionality. Organizations that build flexibility into their value chain design will outperform those still trying to optimize cost at the expense of continuity.

Supply Chain Disruptions

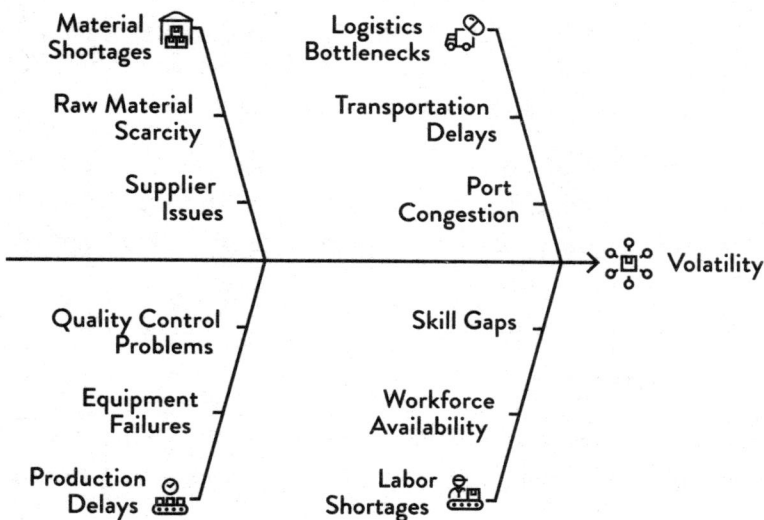

Driver #3:
Demand Volatility

Forecasting demand is no longer a linear exercise. Shifting consumer behavior, economic uncertainty, and global events now render many historical models ineffective. Demand volatility is a strategic constraint.

In ancient Rome, demand spikes were often tied to politics and spectacle. A sudden decree from Caesar to host gladiator games meant a spike in demand for exotic animals, armor, and amphitheater supplies. These surges were unpredictable, and those who could respond quickly profited. Those who couldn't lost favor, contracts, and sometimes heads.[9]

In modern value chains, volatility is even more pronounced. The COVID-19 pandemic reversed decades of predictable trends overnight. Demand surged for home fitness, declined for formal-wear, and realigned again months later. Sustainability shifts, new regulations, and social trends now regularly disrupt baseline forecasts.

To stay ahead, companies are investing in demand-sensing technologies, scenario modeling, and dynamic inventory planning. Agile manufacturing, modular product design, and flexible supplier contracts enable faster response times.

Takeaway: The ability to pivot is no longer a differentiator, it's a baseline requirement. The winners are those who anticipate volatility and embed adaptability into every layer of their value chain.

Driver #4:
Currency Risk

Currency fluctuations can quietly destabilize even the most sophisticated global strategies. As companies expand across borders,

Demand Volatility

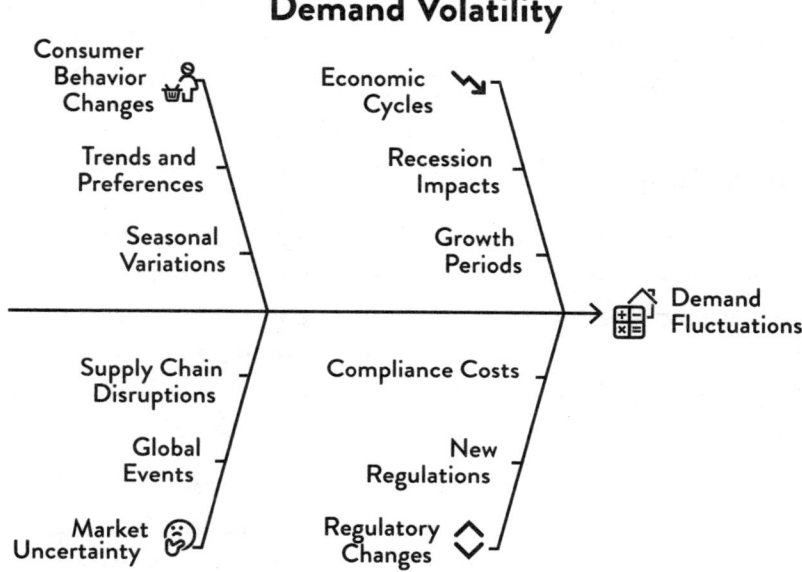

their cost bases and revenue streams are increasingly exposed to exchange-rate volatility.

Even the Romans understood the risks of a weakening currency. As emperors debased their coins, over time merchants began demanding more stable foreign currencies, weakening Rome's monetary authority and complicating trade.[10]

Today, the stakes are Currency, reputational, and strategic. In 2022, the rapid appreciation of the US dollar increased import purchasing power but hurt exporters whose costs remained fixed. Companies operating across multiple currencies saw their margins swing wildly based on external monetary policy decisions.

Sophisticated firms employ hedging strategies, treasury risk modeling, and currency diversification to manage exposure. Too many midsize companies leave this unaddressed until volatility hits—because by then, it's too late.

Takeaway: Currency risk management is a strategic imperative. Value chain leaders must integrate financial volatility planning into sourcing, pricing, and global expansion decisions.

Modern Playbook

Inflation, disruption, volatility, and financial uncertainty aren't new; they're more interconnected, more frequent, and more consequential than ever. Navigating them requires more than operational efficiency. It demands strategic foresight and structural adaptability. Modern value chain individuals must think beyond containment—they must act in terms of competitive leverage.

To lead through inflation, organizations are shifting from reactive cost cutting to proactive value engineering. This includes localized sourcing to reduce logistics exposure, automation to stabilize labor efficiency, and dynamic contract structures that tie pricing to real-time inputs rather than fixed terms.

To withstand disruption, successful firms no longer rely on "Plan B"; they now build portfolios of options. This means geographic supplier diversification, multisource component strategies, and embedded visibility tools to detect bottlenecks before they cascade into crises. Risk is no longer outsourced; it is actively managed through internal governance.

To thrive in volatility, agility is no longer a technical term—it's a cultural one. Flexible production capacity, integrated demand sensing, and cross-functional alignment on reforecasting and response are baseline requirements. Those who invest in fast-turn insights and modular design can shift with the market rather than after it.

To manage currency risk, organizations strengthen ties between finance and operations. This includes deploying sophisticated hedging instruments, scenario-based financial modeling,

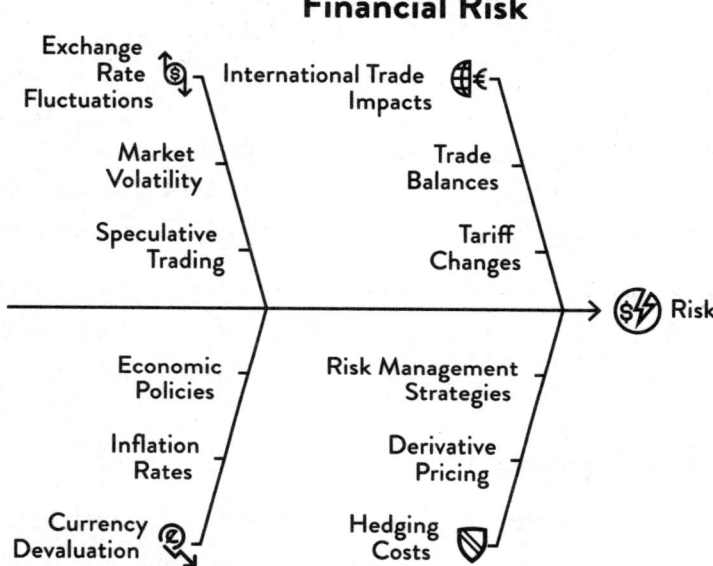

Financial Risk

and pricing strategies that account for currency movements at the planning stage rather than at reconciliation.

These challenges are permanent features of the operating environment. But history is clear: Those who treat volatility as a structural reality, and respond with disciplined flexibility, emerge stronger.

The four drivers aren't simply threats to be minimized; they're accelerators forcing innovation, deepening capabilities, and rewarding strategic clarity. The modern leader's edge doesn't come from avoiding risk; it comes from building systems resilient enough to absorb it.

STRATEGIC LEVERS FOR INFLATION AND DISRUPTION

Economic turbulence isn't new. From Roman emperors to post-COVID multinationals, history shows that organizations don't succeed by avoiding pressure; they succeed by adapting their value chains to absorb, redirect, and eventually capitalize on it.

Below are four key levers that modern teams use to respond strategically—not reactively—to cost inflation, disruption, and volatility.

1. Price Management

Dynamic pricing strategies allow organizations to protect margins in the face of changing input costs and demand signals. Enabled by real-time data and predictive analytics, pricing is now a strategic function—not merely a financial lever.

Merchants along the Silk Road adjusted prices based on distance, route danger, caravan size, and season. It was a decentralized, risk-aware model of dynamic pricing—primitive but effective as an economic strategy.

Amazon adjusts prices millions of times daily using AI-powered algorithms. By analyzing real-time inventory, competitor movements, and purchasing behavior, Amazon can respond to demand shifts and cost pressures without compromising customer trust.

Shared Principles:

- Data-driven decisions

- Embedded risk premiums

- Volume-based discounts

Key Insight: Smart pricing keeps organizations strategically aligned with both market and margin realities.

2. Cost Control

In inflationary environments, margin discipline is a survival trait. Leading organizations combine process optimization with digital tools to monitor and reduce operational inefficiencies at every level of the value chain.

Rome's infrastructure was a master class in standardization and cost control. Uniform road widths, modular design, and specialized labor teams created repeatable models for expansion and maintenance.

Toyota saves hundreds of millions annually through its commitment to continuous improvement. This includes real-time cost tracking, predictive maintenance, energy efficiency, and frontline engagement in cost reduction.

Shared Principles:

- Standardized processes driving efficiency

- Resource reuse and waste minimization

- Cross-functional accountability

Key Insight: Efficiency depends on control. Margins are made—or lost—in the micro-movements of daily operations.

3. Inventory Management

Inventory strategy has shifted from static planning to dynamic response. The goal is no longer simply holding safety stock—it's about aligning working capital with risk, demand, and fulfillment velocity.

To feed its empire, Rome created a vast network of strategically placed grain warehouses. With buffer stocks, seasonal planning, and networked distribution, it ensured continuity in times of crisis.[11]

Walmart maintains a 95 percent in-stock rate across over 10,000 stores while reducing carrying costs by 25 percent, using predictive demand modeling and automated replenishment algorithms.[12]

Shared Principles:

- Demand sensing meets strategic buffering
- Smart warehousing and location planning
- Avoiding working-capital traps without risking service failure

Key Insight: Inventory is neither a cost nor an asset—it's a strategic lever. Mismanage it, and it becomes a liability. Balance provides a competitive edge.

4. Value Chain Redesign

When inflation and disruption reset the rules of engagement, value chains must be reimagined. Teams are no longer making minor adjustments; they're rebuilding for speed, resilience, and regional proximity.

Rome constantly evolved its logistics by establishing alternative routes, regional production hubs, and multimodal transport networks, while maintaining centralized visibility.[13]

In response to pandemic-induced disruptions, Apple restructured its supply base across six countries, reducing average transport distances by 30 percent, increasing supplier redundancy by 40 percent, and embedding AI risk modeling into operations.

Shared Principles:

- Risk distribution through diversification
- Proximity mitigates volatility
- Flexibility becomes a core design principle

Key Insight: Value chains are living systems. To survive disruption, they must evolve continuously.

MODERN TOOLS FOR ECONOMIC NAVIGATION

When economic pressure rises, strategy is only as effective as the tools that execute it. From predictive analytics to financial instruments, today's professionals have more capability at their fingertips than any Roman emperor or Silk Road merchant could imagine.

While the technology is advanced, the purpose remains the same: with clarity, speed, and control.

Here are the essential toolsets modern value chain professionals deploy:

Financial Instruments

In an interconnected global economy, financial tools do more than protect against risk—they enable trade, manage volatility, and preserve profitability across unpredictable cycles.

Today's Tool Kit:

Forward Contracts: Lock in future pricing to reduce volatility and protect margins. This is particularly useful when input costs fluctuate.

Options: Create flexibility without obligation—a vital lever when demand and pricing scenarios remain unclear.

Swaps: Manage exposure by exchanging one type of risk for another—fixed-to-floating interest rates or cross-currency swaps, for example.

Letters of Credit: Ensure trust and payment security in cross-border transactions, reducing credit risk and accelerating deal flow.

Insurance Instruments: Cargo insurance, political risk protection, and business interruption coverage enables continuity even when operations pause or suffer disruption.

Silk Road traders used rudimentary versions of these same tools: letters of credit backed by wealthy banks, risk premiums built into pricing, and partnerships forged with trusted intermediaries to reduce exposure.[14] The principle? You don't need to carry gold if you can carry trust.

Modern financial tools don't remove risk—they give you the agility to control how and where you absorb it.

Analytics and Forecasting

Today's forecasting capabilities are far more reliable than consulting oracles or watching the weather from a grain ship in Alexandria. Yet the challenge remains the same: How do we see the future before it arrives?

Core Capabilities:

Predictive Modeling: Using machine learning AI to forecast demand shifts, pricing swings, and supplier performance.

Scenario Planning: Building "what if" models that simulate disruptions, currency shifts, and regulatory changes.

Risk Assessment Engines: Identifying potential disruptions before they escalate using threat intelligence and exposure mapping.

Cost Trending Dashboards: Tracking movements in input costs, logistics rates, and key drivers that erode margin.

Demand Forecasting Systems: Leveraging behavioral analytics, seasonality, and real-time market data to plan proactively.

Roman leaders depended on grain ledgers, regional reports, and messenger networks to anticipate shortages. Today's dashboards are faster and richer, but they still require interpretation, judgment, and strategic application.

Data doesn't make decisions. Leaders do. But with the right data, they make better ones, faster.

Technology Platforms

If forecasting is the brain of economic navigation, enterprise systems are the nervous system transmitting signals, triggering responses, and coordinating action across complex ecosystems.

Must-Have Systems:

ERP Platforms: Real-time integration of finance, procurement, inventory, and operations for full visibility and speed.

Treasury Management Tools: Optimizing cash flow, managing liquidity, and ensuring funding stability in volatile cycles.

Risk Monitoring Systems: Automating alerts for geopolitical events, supply chain delays, and ESG compliance exposure.

Cost-Tracking Engines: Monitoring cost deviations in real time to allow for immediate intervention.

Performance Analytics Dashboards: Visualize KPIs, productivity metrics, and throughput to inform continuous improvement.

Rome relied on systematized tax collection and distributed authority to govern its far-reaching provinces. The secret was standardization, reporting cadence, and a structured response.

Tools don't replace leadership; they enable it. The best systems make insights timely, decision-making clearer, and action scalable.

Technology doesn't eliminate complexity; it organizes it. The job of the modern value chain leader is to turn noise into insight, risk into resilience, and information into action.

Bridging Strategy and Recovery

Modern tools give us reach, visibility, and speed, but even the best systems cannot fully prevent disruption. They can only position us to respond more effectively when—not if—economic pressures land. And when they do, leaders must shift from optimization to stabilization, from foresight to crisis response. This is where capability meets resilience—where strategies are tested and where recovery becomes a competitive differentiator.

Because as history has shown time and again—from Roman emperors rebuilding scorched cities to corporations restructuring after global shocks—the ability to recover isn't about returning to normal.

It's about coming back stronger.

THE RECOVERY PLAYBOOK

History reminds us that survival is not the endgame; it's the starting line. The Roman Empire didn't endure for centuries because it avoided crisis, but because it had a repeatable model for rebuilding after it. Fires, floods, invasions, and revolts were not merely weathered—they were met with systemic responses: new roads, new laws, new supply lines.

Today's recovery playbook must follow a similar path—from immediate stabilization to long-term transformation. Not reactive scrambling, but structured reinvention.

Phase 1:
Short-Term Survival—Stabilize What Matters

When crisis hits, the goal is continuity. Like a Roman legion under siege, your first move isn't elegant—it's essential.

Core Priorities:

Cash Conservation: Accelerate receivables, stretch payables (strategically), freeze nonessential spending, and prioritize liquidity. Cash isn't just king—it's oxygen.

Targeted Cost Reductions: Eliminate noncritical over-head, reallocate underutilized resources, and cut fat without damaging capability. Think scalpel, not sledgehammer.

Revenue Stabilization: Adjust pricing with precision—not panic. Lean into value-based messaging, reassess customer segmentation, and preserve profitable segments over volume.

Inventory Rationalization: Liquidate slow movers, reassess safety stock thresholds, and refine replenishment logic to free up working capital without jeopardizing service levels.

Survival mode is about clarity, not control. Focus on what moves the needle now. Delay the rest.

Phase 2:
Medium-Term Adaptation—Build Back Stronger

Once the immediate threat is stabilized, shift focus to strengthening operational capacity and reducing systemic vulnerabilities.

Strategic Levers

Process Optimization: Streamline workflows, eliminate bottlenecks, and accelerate digitalization. Efficiency is doing it smarter and simpler.

Supplier Diversification: Rebuild the supply base to include geographic and functional redundancy. Vet alternatives before you need them. Relationships forged now will become your future advantage.

Technology Investment: Upgrade analytics, automate routine tasks, and integrate disconnected systems. Resilience is built on speed of insight and precision of execution.

Contract Realignment: Renegotiate terms that reflect new realities, not outdated assumptions. Flexibility, performance-based triggers, and shared risk incentives should be front and center.

Adaptation is the design of what comes next.

Phase 3:
Long-Term Transformation—Redesign for the Next Normal

Crises reveal what's brittle and also create permission for change. The most successful organizations use recovery windows to do more than bounce back; they leap forward.

Transformational Strategies:

Business Model Innovation: Reevaluate core offerings, customer channels, and revenue structure. Find new relevance, not just efficiency.

Value Chain Redesign: Re-map flows for agility and risk dispersion. Regional hubs, circular models, and strategic reshoring are no longer experiments—they're business imperatives.

Strategic Alliances: Formalize new partnerships and platforms that expand capacity, drive innovation, or share market access. Collaboration is now a multiplier.

Market Repositioning: Refine your value proposition, explore underserved segments, and shift toward where future profit pools will emerge—not where they've already been.

Long-term recovery isn't about returning to where you were. It's about building the capabilities to lead in what comes next.

BOTTOM LINE:
RESILIENCE BY DESIGN

Inflation, volatility, and disruption are enduring conditions woven into the fabric of global trade. What separates those who falter from those who lead is not immunity from pressure but the systems they build to withstand and evolve through it.

Rome didn't collapse from a single cataclysmic event—it fractured under the weight of delayed decisions and rigid systems. The East India Company didn't fail from poor planning—it failed from ignoring warning signs and eroding the partnerships that once made it powerful.

In today's world, leaders don't have the luxury of passivity. They must think ahead, build depth into their value chains, and adopt tools that translate volatility into velocity.

This chapter isn't a checklist. It's a blueprint: for how to lead through inflation without chasing margins, how to absorb disruption without pausing operations, and how to turn economic friction into forward motion.

Resiliency is no longer about weathering impact.

It's about integrating foresight, governance, and adaptability into the very architecture of how you operate.

And if history has taught us anything, it's this: The winners aren't always the strongest. They're the ones who are built to bend and still hold form.

CHAPTER 8

WHAT TO MEASURE

The Roman legions didn't march without maps, and merchants on the Silk Road didn't travel without ledgers.[1] In every era, leaders have relied on measurement to navigate uncertainty, maintain control, and decide where to place their next bet. Without reliable measures, even the most powerful empires or modern corporations are simply steering blind.

In ancient Rome, measurement was more than counting coins or bushels of grain. It was a system of accountability. Governors reported tax revenues in precise tallies; quartermasters tracked rations to the last loaf, and military engineers measured every road so repairs could be forecast before collapse.[2] These metrics didn't exist out of curiosity; they were required for survival.

Today's value chain teams face the same imperative but with infinitely more complexity. Instead of grain and denarii, they're tracking lead times, defect rates, carbon footprints, customer churn, and cash conversion cycles, often across dozens of countries and thousands of suppliers. Yet the principle is unchanged:

What you measure shapes what you manage, and what you manage shapes whether you win or lose.

It's not as easy as you may think. Real danger lies in measuring the wrong things—or worse, drowning in data without extracting the insights that actually drive performance. Rome's downfall was hastened in part by metrics that masked problems: inflated grain inventories, delayed military reports, and tax receipts that painted an overly rosy picture of provincial stability.[3] In modern terms, that's the quarterly report that hides operational risk behind revenue growth, or the KPI dashboard that looks impressive but fails to predict the next disruption.

In this chapter, we'll explore how to identify the measures that matter as well as the metrics that serve as both early warning systems and levers of competitive advantage. We'll draw on history, from Roman logistics to East India Company trade records, and modern examples from companies that have mastered the art of measurement for resilience and growth.

Because in value chains, measurement isn't merely a management tool.

It's the compass.

THE SEVEN DEADLY SINS OF VALUE CHAIN METRICS

The Romans had a saying: *Quidquid recipitur, recipitur ad modum recipientis*—"What is received is received according to the receiver's measure." In other words, the value of information depends entirely on how you collect it, interpret it, and act on it. Measurement has always been a double-edged sword: It can sharpen decision-making, or lead teams astray.

History is littered with examples of measurement gone wrong. Roman governors sometimes inflated grain counts to appear more competent, only for shortages to spark unrest when the reported failed to match the real one. The East India Company, obsessed with tonnage shipped rather than profitability, often moved goods at a loss just to hit volume targets.[4] In both cases, the problem wasn't the absence of data but the pursuit of the wrong data, or blindly trusting numbers divorced from reality.

Modern organizations fall into the same traps. Dashboards glow with KPIs that look impressive in board meetings but fail to capture true performance drivers. Targets are hit while customers defect. Metrics improve while margins erode. In the rush to quantify everything, leaders sometimes forget the golden rule of measurement: If you measure the wrong thing, you get the wrong behavior and you might not realize it until the damage is done.

That's why this section will explore the Seven Deadly Sins of Value Chain Measurement, the most common mistakes organizations make when deciding what to track and how to interpret it. Each "sin" is drawn from history and remains alive in modern business, a reminder that the dangers of poor measurement have remained stubbornly consistent for millennia.

Sin #1:
Vanity Metrics

The first and most seductive sin of measurement is the pursuit of numbers that look good but don't help make better decisions—or worse, that guide you toward the wrong ones. It's an ancient temptation—remember Narcissus, who fell in love with his own reflection?[5] Some metrics are superficially attractive and just as dangerous. I call these *vanity metrics*—things tracked because they look good and make us feel productive . . . even though they don't reflect what really matters or what is really happening.

Modern businesses face the same danger when they chase "vanity metrics"—figures that look impressive in presentations but fail to reflect actual health or strategic progress. A retailer might celebrate year-over-year sales growth without acknowledging shrinking margins. A manufacturer might track units produced without factoring in defect rates or warranty claims. Digital businesses, in particular, are prone to showcasing web traffic, follower counts, or app downloads without measuring conversion, retention, or lifetime value.

The problem with vanity metrics isn't just that they mislead others, it's that they mislead the decision-makers themselves. Leaders who anchor decisions to superficial measures risk directing resources toward appearance rather than impact. This creates a dangerous feedback loop where the organization optimizes for optics while underlying performance erodes.

The antidote is disciplined metric selection. Every measure should be tied to a clear business outcome, operational driver, or strategic priority. In governance terms, this means identifying the metrics that influence, not merely indicate performance, ensuring they are reviewed alongside context and qualitative insight.

Because in value chains, as in empire building, the wrong measures won't just fail to guide you; they'll actively steer you off course—and, the more impressive they look, the faster they'll take you there.

Common Manifestations

Vanity metrics creep into organizations quietly, often hiding in plain sight on dashboards and reports. They tend to reward appearance over impact, creating a false sense of achievement. One of the most common examples is tracking total revenue without considering profitability, as if size alone signals success.

Without the context of margins, warranty claims, and customer service costs, growth can be nothing more than an illusion.

Another example is celebrating order volume without accounting for returns, especially when returns or issues occur months or years after the original revenue was accounted for. It's the equivalent of counting wedding guests without noticing who stayed for dinner or who slipped out early. Similarly, measuring gross shipments instead of perfect order fulfillment favors quantity over quality—a trade-off that erodes customer trust over time.

In the digital world, focusing on social media followers instead of customer satisfaction is a classic trap. Likes and clicks can create the illusion of popularity, but they don't necessarily translate into brand loyalty or revenue. The same applies internally when leaders highlight head count growth instead of productivity. More people in the room doesn't necessarily guarantee better results; sometimes, it just increases the noise.

Looking Good—The Perils of Pretty Numbers:

Risk	Why It's Dangerous	Prevention Strategy
Metrics without business linkage	Consumes resources and tracks numbers that don't influence outcomes	Link every metric directly to a tangible business objective: profitability, retention, or efficiency
Quantity over quality	Encourages output at the expense of performance and customer satisfaction	Pair output measures with quality or satisfaction metrics to ensure accuracy

Risk	Why It's Dangerous	Prevention Strategy
Customer-irrelevant measures	Misses the indicators that drive loyalty, advocacy, and repeat business	Measure what matters most to customers and align those measures with long-term profitability
Metrics that never change	Creates a false sense of stability and hides emerging risks or declines	Challenge consistently "good" metrics; validate their relevance and accuracy regularly
Avoiding uncomfortable truths	Delays addressing operational or strategic weaknesses	Seek metrics that reveal problems early and act on them transparently

Avoiding vanity metrics is as much about discipline as it is about curiosity. The right measures illuminate reality; the wrong ones distort it. By linking metrics to meaningful outcomes, balancing quantity with quality, and leaning into uncomfortable truths, leaders create an information system that drives real improvement rather than hollow wins.

But eliminating vanity metrics is only the first step. Even the best-designed measures can fail if they're collected inconsistently, interpreted without context, or built on unreliable data. That brings us to the second sin, one that has undermined empires, collapsed trade networks, and derailed billion-dollar strategies.

Sin #2:
Analysis Paralysis

A measure is only as good as the integrity of the data behind it. Inconsistent or unreliable data turns even the best-designed metrics into misleading signals—like navigating north with a Jack Sparrow compass that only shows you the direction of your heart's desire.

The East India Company learned this the hard way. Operating across vast distances from London to Bengal, they relied on ship captains, local agents, and regional governors to report trade volumes, commodity prices, and delivery times. But the methods for recording and transmitting this information were anything but consistent. In some ports, officials measured goods by weight; in others, by volume; and in still others, by "bales" of varying size. Time lags in communication meant that prices were often outdated by the time they reached London, and political incentives led some regional offices to inflate or downplay figures to secure more favorable terms from headquarters. Strategic decisions, from pricing opium to allocating naval escorts, were often made on data that was partial, contradictory, or weeks out of date.[6]

Modern organizations face the same challenge when different business units, regions, or supply chain partners operate with conflicting definitions, reporting standards, and timelines. One supplier may report "on-time" delivery when the goods leave their dock, while the customer defines it as arrival at the final destination. Sales teams might count a deal as "closed" when contracts are signed, while finance records it only when payment clears. These inconsistencies create a dangerous illusion of comparability.

The risk is clear: Leaders assume they're working with a unified picture, when in reality, the data is stitched together from incompatible sources. This erodes trust in reporting, slows decision-making, and leads to costly strategic missteps.

Common Manifestations

Data inconsistency often begins innocently enough. Perhaps it's a regional office using a slightly different reporting format, a supplier tracking delivery dates differently than the buyer, or a warehouse counting "units" in ways that don't align with corporate definitions. Over time, these small differences compound into a major problem: numbers that appear comparable but are not measuring the same thing.

One of the most common issues is reporting on different cycles. Sales may report monthly, production weekly, and logistics daily, making it difficult to align trends or spot issues in real time.

Manual processes also contribute to unreliable data. Human-entered figures, often based on judgment calls or incomplete information, are prone to error. Clean and reliable master data is essential. Without consistent data-cleaning and validation, these inaccuracies slip into reports and dashboards, where they are mistaken for truth.

Finally, incompatible systems, where one unit measures in pounds, another in kilograms, and another in container counts, can make aggregation and analysis a slow, error-prone process.

These manifestations don't just cause reporting headaches; they distort the leader's view of reality. And in decision-making, a distorted picture can be more dangerous than no picture at all.

Analysis Paralysis—Data Risks and Safeguards:

Risk	Why It's Dangerous	Prevention Strategy
Different definitions of the same metric	Creates false comparisons and misaligns performance assessments	Establish a data governance framework with standardized metrics
Inconsistent reporting intervals	Prevents accurate trend analysis and timely interventions	Align reporting cycles across all business units and partners
Manual, error-prone collection	Introduces inaccuracies that compound over time	Automate data capture wherever possible; use validation checks
Poor data quality control	Allows errors, duplicates, and gaps to persist	Implement centralized data-cleaning protocols and audit processes
Siloed or incompatible systems	Limits visibility and slows decision-making	Integrate systems or use middleware to ensure data compatibility

The lesson is timeless: Without consistent, reliable data, even the most sophisticated measurement system becomes a guessing game. The East India Company's far-flung operations were undermined not by a lack of reports but by the lack of comparability between them. Modern leaders face the same risk—making high-stake decisions on a patchwork of mismatched metrics.

Next, we'll turn to the third sin—one that isn't about *how* you collect data but about *what* you choose to leave out.

Sin #3:
When Good Metrics Drive Bad Behavior

Not everything that matters can be counted, and not everything that can be counted matters. The third sin of measurement is focusing so heavily on what's easily quantifiable that leaders often overlook the intangible factors that often determine long-term success or failure.

Silk Road merchants understood this all too well. Caravan leaders meticulously tracked quantities of silk, spices, and precious metals, but the most decisive factors in a journey's success were often intangible: trust among trading partners, the reliability of guides, the strength of local alliances, and the perceived fairness of deals. A merchant could have a warehouse full of goods and a detailed inventory yet still fail if their reputation suffered in a key city-state or if word spread that their caravan mistreated local intermediaries. These soft factors didn't appear on shipping manifests, but they could make or break a trade network.[7]

Modern organizations fall into the same trap when they prioritize operational and financial KPIs while sidelining indicators of culture, customer sentiment, brand equity, or innovation capacity. These intangibles may be harder to measure, but ignoring them can leave a company blind to brewing risks. A manufacturer might track production efficiency to the second but fail to measure employee engagement, only to watch key talent flee and productivity collapse. A retailer might monitor sales per square foot while missing a steady decline in customer loyalty, masked by one-off promotions.

Common Manifestations

One of the most frequent signs of this sin is overreliance on "hard" performance metrics without complementary qualitative or proxy measures. For example, companies may track customer acquisition cost (CAC) but ignore customer lifetime value (CLV). Similarly, they might measure product defect rates while overlooking design quality or user satisfaction, both of which directly influence repeat purchases.

Another manifestation is short-termism, focusing exclusively on quarterly results without tracking leading indicators of future performance, such as innovation pipeline strength, partnership quality, or workforce skills development. This tunnel vision creates a dangerous gap: Leaders may be winning the current quarter while quietly undermining their competitiveness in the next.

Finally, cultural and reputational blind spots emerge when organizations fail to measure what's being said about them in the market or how employees truly feel about current leadership Without these insights, risks can grow unchecked until they manifest as attrition, employee and customer churn, or public relations crises.

When Good Metrics Drive Bad Behavior— Intangibles Ignored, Risks Exposed:

Risk	Why It's Dangerous	Prevention Strategy
Overreliance on hard metrics	Misses performance drivers that don't show up in purely quantitative measures	Pair operational KPIs with qualitative and proxy measures for balance
Short-term performance fixation	Sacrifices long-term health for short-term wins	Track leading indicators alongside lagging results to ensure sustainability

Risk	Why It's Dangerous	Prevention Strategy
Ignoring culture and sentiment	Risks employee disengagement and customer attrition	Incorporate engagement surveys, sentiment analysis, and stakeholder feedback loops
Reputation as a blind spot	Public perception shifts can impact sales and partnerships before they appear in financials	Monitor brand sentiment and media mentions as part of standard reporting
Innovation gaps	Fails to anticipate competitive threats or market changes	Measure R&D pipeline, speed-to-market, and cross-functional collaboration rates
Partnership quality overlooked	Weak alliances erode long-term competitive advantage	Develop metrics for partner engagement, mutual value creation, and collaboration effectiveness

The Silk Road prospered not only on goods exchanged but also on who earned trust and maintained relationships. Merchants who ignored the intangible forces behind trade often found themselves locked out of markets or paying steep premiums to rebuild credibility. Modern professionals face the same reality: Measurement must go beyond the obvious and into the forces that sustain performance over time. Which brings us to the fourth sin, one that turns even the right metrics into the wrong conclusions.

Sin #4:
Silo Mentality

Having the right data doesn't guarantee the right decision. The fourth sin of measurement is misinterpreting the numbers by mistaking correlation for causation, ignoring context, or oversimplifying complex dynamics. This is where leaders can have accurate, timely data—and still head out in exactly the wrong direction.

A cautionary tale comes from early maritime exploration. In the sixteenth century, Portuguese spice traders meticulously tracked ship arrival times and cargo volumes from the East Indies. When a sudden surge in late arrivals coincided with increased piracy in the Indian Ocean, traders concluded piracy was solely to blame. In reality, weather patterns and navigational errors were equally significant factors, but these went unmeasured and unconsidered. Acting on an incomplete diagnosis, they diverted naval escorts to the busiest trade routes, leaving other lanes vulnerable and unintentionally increasing overall losses.[8]

Modern businesses repeat this mistake when they jump to conclusions based on surface-level patterns. A retailer might see sales spike after a social media campaign and assume the campaign caused it, ignoring a concurrent competitor stockout that drove customers their way. A manufacturer might blame a drop in productivity solely on equipment downtime, overlooking rising turnover in skilled staff. Misinterpretation isn't merely a technical problem; it's a governance problem, because it reflects a failure to challenge assumptions and validate conclusions before acting.

Common Manifestations

One clear sign of this sin is over-attributing results to a single cause. Complex systems rarely have one driver, yet performance reviews and board updates often highlight a single "reason" for success or failure. Another is confirmation bias, where individuals interpret data in ways that validate their preexisting beliefs, filtering out contradictory evidence.

Misinterpretation can also occur when metrics are viewed in isolation without context or comparative benchmarks. A 10 percent improvement in on-time delivery sounds great—until you learn competitors improved by 20 percent in the same period. Finally, ignoring lagging effects can lead to misjudging the timing between cause and effect, prompting premature changes or missed opportunities.

Silo Mentality—Partial Metrics, Broken Systems:

Risk	Why It's Dangerous	Prevention Strategy
Over-attributing to a single cause	Leads to incomplete solutions and misdirected resources	Use multifactor analysis to identify all contributing factors
Confirmation bias	Reinforces flawed assumptions and blocks corrective action	Challenge interpretations with comprehensive reviews and peer validation
Metrics without context	Makes performance appear better or worse than reality	Pair metrics with benchmarks, historical trends, and competitor comparisons

Risk	Why It's Dangerous	Prevention Strategy
Ignoring lagging effects	Misaligns actions with true cause-and-effect timing	Map timelines between inputs and outcomes; adjust decision windows accordingly
Isolated decision-making	Risks groupthink and limited perspectives	Involve cross-functional teams in interpreting results
Lack of scenario testing	Fails to explore alternate explanations for the same data	Run "what else could explain this?" exercises before finalizing conclusions

Misinterpreting data can be more dangerous than having no data at all—it leads to confident, well-resourced decisions that are wrong from the start. Whether on the high seas of the spice trade or in today's global markets, the real skill is not simply collecting metrics but interpreting them with discipline and context. And that brings us to the fifth sin, one rooted in how we choose which data to prioritize.

Sin #5:
The Rearview Mirror

Lagging indicators tell you what has already happened. They are essential for measuring outcomes but dangerous when they dominate decision-making without the balance of leading indicators that can signal what's coming next. The fifth sin of measurement is relying too heavily on the rearview mirror to steer the organization forward.

The Roman Empire, despite its engineering brilliance, was not immune to this mistake. Provincial governors reported harvest yields, tax revenues, and completed infrastructure projects back to Rome, all lagging measures of provincial stability and productivity. Decisions about troop deployments, trade priorities, and tax rates were often based on these past results. But by the time the reports arrived and were acted on, conditions in the provinces could have changed drastically.[9]

Modern companies fall into the same trap when they overemphasize past sales performance, or last year's market share, without pairing them with forward-looking indicators. A tech company might celebrate a strong Q4 without noticing a shrinking pipeline for the next two quarters. A manufacturer might focus on last month's output while ignoring early signs of supplier financial instability or raw material shortages.

Common Manifestations

Overreliance on lagging indicators often shows up as decision-making that reacts rather than anticipates. Leaders wait for a metric to confirm a trend before acting, missing the window for early intervention. It also appears in performance reviews that are heavily weighted toward past results, which can reward short-term wins that undermine long-term strategy.

Another manifestation is forecasting based primarily on historical averages, a method that assumes future conditions will mirror the past. In volatile markets or rapidly changing geopolitical environments, this approach is risky at best and disastrous at worst. Finally, organizations may underinvest in data that is harder to collect, such as market sentiment, early-stage sales activity, or R&D progress, leaving them blind to catastrophic shifts in competitive position.

Rear-View Mirror—Lagging Indicators and Lost Foresight:

Risk	Why It's Dangerous	Prevention Strategy
past results	Locks strategy to outdated conditions	Pair lagging metrics with leading indicators for a balanced view
Slow reaction to change	Misses early opportunities or warning signs	Build rapid-feedback systems for near-real-time data collection
Rewarding short-term wins	Encourages decisions that harm long-term health	Include forward-looking goals and innovation metrics in performance reviews
Forecasting by historical average	Assumes stability in unstable markets	Use scenario planning and dynamic forecasting models
Neglecting hard-to-measure indicators	Leaves blind spots in strategic planning	Invest in tools and methods to capture early signals, even if imperfect
Overconfidence in past success	Reduces urgency to innovate or adapt	Regularly stress-test strategy against emerging trends and threats

Lagging indicators are invaluable for confirming results but disastrous when they become the sole compass for future action. Rome learned that last year's abundant harvests or completed aqueducts said nothing about this year's droughts, unrest, or shifting alliances. Modern leaders face the same reality: Yesterday's success offers no guarantee of tomorrow's stability. Which brings us to the sixth sin, one that's less about the timeline of the data and more about whether you're even looking in the right direction.

Sin #6:
False Precision

Numbers can create an aura of certainty. The sixth sin of measurement is mistaking numerical detail for accuracy and treating a number as absolute simply because it's presented with confidence, decimal points, or elaborate calculations. This "illusion of precision" can mislead decision-makers into overestimating the reliability of their data and underestimating the uncertainty behind it.

The East India Company provides a textbook example. From London headquarters to far-flung trading posts, clerks produced exquisitely detailed ledgers tracking shipments down to the last pound of tea or bale of cotton. These records gave directors the comforting impression that they had total visibility into operations. But beneath the precision lay shaky foundations—weights and measures varied between ports, goods were often lost or "misplaced" en route, and some regional agents inflated figures to protect their reputations or secure more resources. Strategic decisions about fleet deployment, pricing, and contract terms were often made with numbers that looked scientific but were riddled with inaccuracies.[10]

Modern corporations fall into the same trap when they rely on models, dashboards, and analytics outputs without questioning the data quality, assumptions, or margin of error. Forecasts showing sales growth to two decimal places can mask the fact that the underlying survey sample was too small, outdated, or biased. Supply chain simulations might model shipment times down to the hour while ignoring customs clearance delays or political disruptions. In both cases, leaders confuse the *presentation* of precision with the *reality* of accuracy.

Common Manifestations

One common sign of this sin is overconfidence in model outputs without stress-testing the assumptions behind them. Another is overuse of decimal places, which implies a level of certainty the data cannot actually support. Businesses may also ignore margins of error entirely, presenting forecasts and KPIs as absolute truths rather than probability ranges.

On the corporate side, complexity bias, where leaders value a metric more because it's the product of an intricate model, can lead to a dangerous overreliance on tools rather than judgment. Finally, a lack of transparency about data sources and methods can make flawed precision harder to detect until the consequences hit.

False Precision—When Numbers Deceive:

Risk	Why It's Dangerous	Prevention Strategy
Overconfidence in model outputs	Masks uncertainty and leads to high-stake errors	Require clear documentation of assumptions and sensitivity analysis
Misleading decimals	Creates false perception of accuracy	Round to a level that reflects true data reliabilit
Ignoring margins of error	Overstates certainty and limits contingency planning	Include error ranges and confidence intervals in all reporting

Risk	Why It's Dangerous	Prevention Strategy
Complexity bias	Overvalues elaborate outputs over simpler, more reliable measures	Challenge complex results with simple validation checks
Opaque data sources	Hides potential flaws in inputs	Demand transparency in sourcing, transformation, and calculation methods
Failure to stress-test metrics	Leaves organizations unprepared for outlier events	Regularly test metrics under different scenarios to gauge robustness

The East India Company learned, often too late, that beautiful ledgers could hide ugly realities. Modern companies risk the same fate when they let clean spreadsheets or sophisticated dashboards replace healthy skepticism. Numbers may speak, but without context, they can also lie convincingly. Which brings us to the final sin, one that isn't about the accuracy of your measures but about the discipline to keep measuring at all.

Sin #7:
Set It and Forget It

Even the Romans updated their maps as their empire grew. Your metrics should evolve too. Taking a lazy, *set-and-forget* approach with your metrics ensures you'll be dining on bad decisions made with spoiled data sometime in your future.

The final sin of measurement isn't ignoring data—it's continuing to measure things that no longer matter. Metrics that once served as useful indicators can outlive their relevance, quietly draining time, resources, and attention. The danger is subtle: Teams keep producing reports, leaders may or may not be reviewing them, and no one stops to ask, "Why are we still measuring this?"

The Roman Empire faced this problem in its later years. Census and tax systems were designed for an era of expansion, measuring land ownership and agricultural output as the primary signs of prosperity. But as Rome urbanized and trade became highly reliant on imports, these measures told less and less about the actual economic health of the empire.[11] By continuing to focus on outdated indicators, Rome missed the signals of declining GDP, rising dependency on imports, and shifting military threats, both internally and externally.

Modern organizations fall into the same trap when they measure because "we've always measured that." A manufacturing company might still track machine uptime as its key productivity even after automation has shifted the real bottleneck to supply chain lead times. A retailer might focus on store foot traffic long after e-commerce has become the dominant sales channel. Corporate reports fill with pages of legacy KPIs that no longer link to strategic priorities, giving the illusion of control while hiding real performance drivers.

Common Manifestations

One telltale sign of this sin is reporting inertia, where KPIs survive not because they're valuable but because removing them feels politically risky or administratively inconvenient. Another is distraction by tradition, where leadership continues to review metrics out of habit even when they no longer influence decision-making.

Obsolete metrics also lead to misaligned incentives, rewarding teams for improving numbers that no longer move the organization forward. And because legacy KPIs are often embedded in systems and reports, they can persist for years without challenge, crowding out newer, more relevant measures.

Set and Forget—Outdated Metrics, Hidden Risks:

Risk	Why It's Dangerous	Prevention Strategy
Reporting inertia	Wastes resources and executive attention	Conduct annual KPI audits to retire metrics with no strategic link
Misaligned incentives	Encourages effort in the wrong areas	Align KPIs with current business objectives and competitive realities
Metric dilution	Important metrics get lost in irrelevant noise	Prioritize a focused set of high-value metrics
Organizational complacency	Avoids questioning existing systems	Build a culture that challenges the "we've always measured this" mindset
Slow adaptation	Metrics lag behind strategic pivots	Review KPIs after major market, product, or operating model changes
Hidden opportunity cost	Resources are tied up maintaining low-value metrics	Reallocate analysis capacity to emerging priorities and future indicators

Rome's fixation on outdated indicators blinded it to the real shifts undermining its power. Modern companies risk the same fate when they mistake longevity for value in their measurement systems. A truly effective measurement strategy is as much about knowing what to stop measuring as it is about knowing what to start.

MODERN MEASUREMENT TOOLS

In the ancient world, successful empires built systems to track what was moving across them. Roman census rolls, Chinese imperial grain ledgers, and Silk Road merchant tallies were the original "business intelligence" platforms. They were imperfect, but they gave leaders visibility and a basis for action.[12]

Today's organizations have exponentially more data—but that doesn't automatically translate into better decisions. The tools have evolved from clay tablets and scrolls to cloud platforms and AI dashboards, yet the goal remains the same: Turn information into insight, and insight into advantage.

Modern measurement tools fall into three broad categories.

CATEGORY 1:
CORE SYSTEMS

Every measurement strategy begins with a foundation: the systems and processes that capture, store, and structure operational and financial data.

In ancient Rome, this backbone was the census and tax roll system. Conducted every five years, it was designed to catalog the empire's people, land, and assets, a process that allowed for resource allocation, tax planning, and military conscription. It was not perfect, since data could be outdated by the time it reached the capital, but it created a standardized framework across diverse territories. The East India Company relied on a similar backbone:

Uniform ledger books and double-entry accounting practices were required in every trading post, ensuring that shipments from Bengal could be reconciled with sales in London.[13]

Modern businesses rely on core systems to perform the same essential role: creating a *single source of truth* for operations, finance, and supply chain. But these systems are more than repositories. They define how the business process works, influencing everything from order management to supplier onboarding.

Core System Business Processes

Standardization Across Functions
Core systems enforce a common language for data. In a global manufacturing business, this means "inventory" is calculated the same way in São Paulo as it is in Singapore, eliminating costly misinterpretations.

Governance by Design
Well-configured systems embed compliance checks directly into workflows. Purchase orders can't be issued without approved budgets, and suppliers can't be paid without verification against delivery. This turns governance from a policing function into an automated part of daily operations.

Integration for End-to-End Visibility
By linking finance, procurement, production, and logistics, core systems reveal the ripple effects of decisions. A change in sales forecasts instantly updates production schedules, which then updates supplier order volumes and cash flow projections.

Auditability and Traceability

Like the Roman census rolls that could be referenced decades later, modern ERP and financial systems create a permanent record of decisions, transactions, and approvals, which become invaluable during audits, disputes, or investigations.

Strategic Caution

Core systems are only as good as the processes and discipline that support them. When business units create their own definitions, bypass standard workflows, or treat data entry as an afterthought, the integrity of the entire measurement framework collapses. The result is a system that may look sophisticated on the surface but produces inconsistent, unreliable, or incomplete information.

Common failure points include:

Inconsistent data definitions across regions or departments, leading to conflicting reports.

Workarounds that bypass approval gates or validation checks, eroding governance controls.

Poor change management, where process updates aren't properly communicated or enforced.

Underinvestment in training, leaving teams unaware of how to use the system correctly or why compliance matters.

The fix isn't adding more technology, it's tighter alignment between people, processes, and system. This means embedding data governance policies into standard operating procedures, assigning clear accountability for data quality, and ensuring leaders model the discipline they expect from their teams.

Category 2:
Analytical Engines

If core systems are the backbone of measurement, analytical engines are the brains, turning raw data into understanding, foresight, and strategic direction. They enable leaders to move beyond simply knowing *what happened* to anticipating *what will happen* and deciding *what to do about it*.

The Silk Road offers an early example of applied analytics. Merchants didn't merely track past journeys, they built models in their heads, factoring in seasonal weather, political alliances, risk of banditry, and shifting market demand. These "mental algorithms" shaped decisions about routes, cargo composition, and pricing long before anyone coined the term *analytics*. The difference today is scale, speed, sophistication, and the ability to run thousands of scenarios in seconds rather than weeks.

Analytical Engine Processes

1. **Decision Support at Every Level**
   Analytical tools translate data into actionable insights for different audiences: Executives get strategic trend forecasts, managers get operational performance dashboards, and frontline teams get real-time alerts.

2. **Predictive and Prescriptive Capability**
   Predictive analytics identify likely future outcomes; prescriptive analytics recommends specific actions to influence those outcomes. This shifts measurement from reactive to proactive.

3. **Scenario Planning and Stress-Testing**
   These engines allow leaders to test multiple "what if" scenarios, from raw material shortages to sudden demand spikes, before committing resources.

4. Identifying Leading Indicators

Instead of relying solely on lagging KPIs like revenue or profit, analytics can highlight earlier signals, like supplier capacity changes, customer sentiment shifts, or cost trend modulation that predict future performance.

Strategic Caution

The strength of any analytical engine depends on the quality of its inputs and the clarity of its assumptions. Poor or inconsistent data from core systems will produce misleading outputs, regardless of how advanced the analytics. Equally dangerous is AI "black box" decision-making, when individuals accept model outputs without questioning how the results were derived.

Common pitfalls include:

Garbage in, garbage out—flawed data produces inaccurate insights.

Model overfitting, where tools become too narrowly tailored to past data and fail to adapt to new conditions.

Overconfidence in projections, especially when they're expressed with excessive precision.

Failure to align analytics with strategy, leading to insights that are interesting but irrelevant to future business goals.

Mitigation requires data governance discipline, transparency in model design, and a process for validating outputs against real-world conditions. Analytical engines are powerful, but they are not infallible; they work best when paired with human judgment and business context.

Category 3: Decision Support

Core systems provide the foundation. Analytical engines generate insight. But without effective decision support, even the best intelligence remains unused. Decision support tools bridge the gap between knowing and doing, while enabling leaders to act on insights with speed, accuracy, and coordination.

The Roman military understood this principle well. In active campaigns, commanders relied on a network of scouts, signal towers, and dispatch riders to provide near-real-time updates on enemy movements and supply status. These reports didn't just sit in a ledger—they informed immediate tactical decisions, from troop redeployments to changes in supply routes. In the modern context, decision support systems perform a similar function, turning raw and analyzed data into coordinated, timely action across the organization.

Decision Support Processes

Command and Control
Decision support platforms—from supply chain control towers to enterprise-wide KPI dashboards—allow leaders to monitor performance in real time and initiate immediate course corrections.

Risk Monitoring and Mitigation
Integrated alerts, risk heat maps, and scenario simulations help organizations respond before an issue becomes a disruption.

Cross-Functional Alignment
This ensures finance, operations, procurement, and sales make coordinated decisions based on the same intelligence, reducing the risk of conflicting priorities.

Continuous Improvement

Feedback mechanisms allow organizations to track the impact of decisions and refine processes for greater efficiency over time.

Strategic Caution

Decision support tools are effective only if authority delegation, escalation paths, and accountability are clearly defined. Without governance, tools risk becoming observation posts rather than action centers.

Typical failure points include:

Information overload, where practitioners are flooded with data but lack clarity on which metrics matter most.

Slow response protocols, where insights aren't translated into timely action due to unclear ownership.

Siloed decision-making, where one function acts on its own data without considering enterprise-wide implications.

Lack of post-action review, meaning the organization learns nothing from past decisions.

To avoid these traps, organizations must embed clear decision-making frameworks within their tools, ensure role clarity for all levels of authority, and maintain a culture where decisions are both prompt and reviewable.

From Metrics to Meaning: Turning Numbers into Decisions

The East India Company built a $4.2 trillion empire—in today's terms—without a single spreadsheet. Rome managed an empire spanning three continents with parchment rolls, ink, and disciplined process. Their success wasn't about technology, it was about *what* they measured, *why* they measured it, and *how* they used the results.

Modern teams have tools those empires couldn't dream of, today, measurement systems are only as valuable as the decisions and actions they drive. Here's the modern blueprint.

Step 1:
Define What Matters

Before you measure anything, determine why it matters. A metric without purpose is just noise.

Strategic Alignment: Every measurement must connect directly to your strategic objectives. Ask: Does this metric drive the right behavior? Is it telling us what we need to know or merely what's easy to count?

Stakeholder Relevance: Engage decision-makers at all levels to ensure metrics reflect both operational realities and strategic priorities.

Value Creation Focus: Metrics should contribute to creating or protecting value, not just recording it.

Action Orientation: If a metric can't be linked to a specific decision or corrective action, it doesn't belong on the dashboard.

Step 2:
Build the Framework

Strong metrics need a delivery system that is disciplined, repeatable, and resilient.

Data Collection: Establish consistent, validated data capture processes across all functions. Quality inputs are the foundation for meaningful outputs.

Analysis Methods: Move from raw data to insight with clear, transparent methodologies that practitioners can trust.

Reporting Structures: Design reporting so information flows where it's needed, when it's needed.

Review Processes: Schedule regular reviews to retire outdated measures, refine definitions, and adjust for market or strategy shifts.

Step 3:
Drive Action

The ultimate test of a measurement system is the quality of the decisions it shapes.

Decision Support: Present information in a way that highlights priorities, trade-offs, and urgency.

Performance Improvement: Use metrics to illuminate the "why" behind performance gaps and to direct improvement efforts.

Innovation Stimulus: Identify forward-looking opportunities, not just current performance.

Risk Management: Build in early-warning indicators so teams can act before issues escalate.

THE BOTTOM LINE:
DATA MUST DIRECT, NOT DISTRACT

Across centuries and continents, the leaders who mastered measurement were those who linked it directly to action. They didn't count for the sake of counting—they counted to control, to adapt, and to advance.

In modern value chains, the temptation to track everything is stronger than ever. But more data isn't more insight. The discipline lies in focusing on the few measures that truly shape outcomes, ensuring they are accurate, timely, and tied to strategic priorities.

Avoiding the "Seven Sins" of measurement means building systems where:

Every metric has a purpose and a decision attached to it

Governance and process discipline protect data integrity

Modern tools are harnessed to support strategy, not overwhelm it

Outdated measures are retired before they consume attention and resources

In the end, measurement is a leadership capability. Organizations that measure well know where to go next and how to get there.

CHAPTER 9

GLOBAL EVENTS

Picture an East India Company official in the eighteenth century, quill in hand, drafting a report on why a shipment of spices is weeks late. "Pirates off the Malabar Coast have intercepted the fleet," he writes, "and monsoon rains have flooded the warehouses in Calcutta." Just as he finishes, another courier arrives with worse news: "The famine in Bengal has wiped out the labor force, and our trading posts are in chaos."[1]

This wasn't an isolated incident. For the East India Company, global disruptions were routine: Pirate attacks, climate disasters, political rebellions, and trade embargoes were simply another day at the office. Their ability to navigate these challenges, albeit imperfectly, is a testament to both the resilience and fragility of interconnected value chains. When they succeeded, they wielded unparalleled power; when they failed, the consequences were catastrophic, as seen in the Bengal Famine, where overextension and mismanagement contributed to unimaginable human suffering.[2]

Fast-forward to today, and the parallels are clear. Global events, be they natural disasters, pandemics, or geopolitical conflicts, still wreak havoc on value chains. A single disruption in one corner of the world can cascade across continents, upending everything from raw material sourcing to last-mile delivery. The stakes are high, and the margins for error are razor-thin.

This chapter explores how modern value chains can learn from the past and prepare for the future. You can't prevent global disruptions, but you can build systems that weather the storm. Whether the threat is a pirate or a pandemic, resilience is survival.

GLOBAL DISRUPTION DISRUPTS

When it comes to global events, think of them as four relentless forces capable of reshaping your value chain overnight. They are not abstract "black swan" events, nor are they once-in-a-generation anomalies; they are recurring stress tests that can hit without warning. Each has the power to stop production, reroute supply lines, disrupt demand, and shift competitive advantage in a matter of days.

For senior leaders, the challenge is in preparing systems, relationships, and strategies that can absorb the impact, adapt quickly, and, in some cases, turn disruption into opportunity. These are the moments where value chain resilience is tested in the real world, far beyond the safety of planning documents or quarterly reviews.

The four disruption categories that follow—natural disasters, health crises, geopolitical events, and economic shocks—may look different in cause, but they are identical in effect: They disrupt flow, increase risk, and pressure decision-making speed. Successful organizations share one trait: They treat disruption management as a core competency, not a contingency plan.

Disruption #1:
Natural Disasters

Natural disasters are the most impartial of disruptions because they can strike anywhere, affect anyone, and often arrive with little or no warning. Their impact is rarely contained within a single location; damage to one link in the value chain can ripple globally through suppliers, customers, and markets.

Recent events highlight just how fast those ripples can spread:

Earthquakes: Japan's 2024 Noto Peninsula earthquake caused an estimated $10 billion in damage, disrupting infrastructure, agriculture, aquaculture, and tourism, with insured losses nearing $2 billion.[3]

Hurricanes: Hurricane Helene (2024) left $75 billion in damages, hitting North Carolina, Florida's Big Bend, and the Gulf Coast hardest—crippling manufacturing, agriculture, and transport networks.[4]

Floods: In 2024, widespread flooding in China caused $15.6 billion in economic losses, overwhelming local infrastructure.[5]

Volcanic Eruptions: Iceland's Sundhnúksgígar eruption (2024) lasted fifty-four days, damaging infrastructure and causing extensive land degradation.[6]

Climate Change: From 1980 to 2024, the US averaged twenty-three major weather-related disasters annually in its most recent five-year span, totaling nearly $3 trillion in losses. The insurance industry has already begun retreating from high-risk zones like parts of Florida, with other hurricane-prone states likely to follow.[7]

What makes natural disasters particularly challenging is their compound effect: Physical damage coincides with transport delays, supplier downtime, workforce displacement, and sudden spikes in demand for replacement goods. As climate volatility increases, even companies located far from disaster zones must anticipate secondary impacts, such as input shortages, logistics bottlenecks, or sudden market shifts.

Strategic Response:

1. **Redundancy:** Toyota reduced geographic concentration by diversifying suppliers and relocating production to less disaster-prone areas.

2. **Risk Mapping:** UPS uses advanced analytics to pinpoint high-risk regions and pre-plan alternative routing.

3. **Disaster Recovery Planning:** China has invested heavily in upgrading dams and reservoirs and pioneering "Sponge Cities" that utilize deltas and plant vegetation to absorb and redirect floodwaters naturally.

Natural disasters are inevitable; however, catastrophic operational failure doesn't have to be. The companies that fare best treat disaster readiness as part of core operations, not as a side activity for "when something happens."

Disruption #2: Health Crises

Health crises prove that the smallest organisms can bring the largest economies to a standstill. The speed of transmission, the scope of impact, and the unpredictability of outbreaks make health events uniquely destabilizing for value chains. They disrupt production and logistics while affecting workforce availability, regulatory environments, and consumer behavior in ways that can persist long after the initial crisis.

Recent history offers stark examples:

Pandemics: COVID-19 cost the global economy $28 trillion. Container shipping rates surged 500 percent, lead times doubled, and shortages hit critical sectors like semiconductors and medical supplies[8]

Regional Outbreaks: The 2003 SARS outbreak cost $40 billion primarily through disruptions to Asia's trade and travel industries, serving as an early warning of the fragility of interconnected systems[9]

Health Regulations: During COVID-19, strict port sanitation and quarantine measures caused delays of up to ten days for goods arriving in Shanghai[10]

Worker Safety: In 2020, US meatpacking plants became COVID-19 hotspots, triggering closures that pushed beef and pork prices up by 25 to 40 percent[11]

Supply Chain Hygiene: The 2018 romaine lettuce E. coli outbreak in the US caused at least $300 million in losses across the food industry.[12]

Health crises hit value chains in waves—the first impacts operations directly, and subsequent waves emerge from regulatory changes, shifting consumer demand, and reputational risks. The absence of preparedness compounds these effects, turning short-term shocks into long-term setbacks.

Strategic Response:

Health Protocols: Amazon kept warehouses running during COVID-19 by introducing temperature checks, sanitation stations, and rapid-response hygiene measures

Inventory Reserves: Singapore maintains a six-month stockpile of essential medical supplies to ensure continuity during global shortages[13]

Agile Operations: Manufacturers rapidly repurposed production lines to produce vaccines, proving the competitive advantage of flexible manufacturing setups.

Health crises are not merely medical events—they are full-spectrum business disruptions. Leaders who integrate health-risk planning into operational strategy are better equipped to protect both people and performance when the next outbreak occurs.

Disruption #3: Geopolitical Events

Geopolitical shifts can alter trade flows, reshape sourcing strategies, and disrupt markets overnight. Unlike natural disasters or health crises, these disruptions are often rooted in policy decisions, regulatory changes, or conflict, and they can last years instead of weeks. Their effects ripple beyond immediate trade routes, influencing everything from input costs to investment decisions.

Recent disruptions illustrate the scale and speed of impact:

Trade Wars: The US-China trade war (starting 2018) placed tariffs on $550 billion in goods, forcing companies like Apple to shift production out of China. Vietnam saw a 25 percent increase in manufacturing investment as companies diversified[14]

Sanctions: Sanctions on Russia in 2022 disrupted $330 billion in annual trade, particularly in energy and agriculture, with European gas prices spiking 40 percent[15]

Border Closures: Brexit added £7 billion annually in customs costs for UK businesses, while shipping times between the UK and EU rose by 40 percent[16]

Regulatory Shifts: The EU's 2021 Green Deal imposed strict environmental requirements, pushing industries such as automotive to invest billions in compliance[17]

Political Instability: The Arab Spring (2010 to 2014) caused disruptions in oil-producing nations, driving crude prices up 25 percent in just six months.[18]

Geopolitical events often force value chains to confront a trade-off between stability and cost efficiency. Long-standing supplier relationships may need to be reconsidered, and market entry strategies recalibrated, to account for shifting alliances or emerging trade barriers.

Strategic Response:

Scenario Planning: Shell's "Energy Scenarios" framework models potential geopolitical outcomes to guide investment and operational decisions

Diversification: Dell reduced reliance on China by expanding sourcing from India and Southeast Asia, avoiding the full brunt of tariffs[19]

Intelligence Networks: DHL's geopolitical monitoring teams track real-time developments to reroute shipments and adapt operations on short notice.[20]

Geopolitical events can permanently alter the global map of production and distribution. Organizations that build political risk monitoring into their governance models gain the agility to adapt before these shifts become crises.

Disruption #4:
Economic Shocks

Economic shocks can cascade through value chains at alarming speed. A sudden shift in financial conditions, whether sparked by a market crash, a currency collapse, or a resource shortage, can dry up capital, disrupt pricing, and make previously viable operations unsustainable. These shocks rarely stay confined to the financial sector; they spill over into procurement decisions, inventory levels, and strategic investments.

Recent examples show how quickly these shocks can materialize:

Financial Crises: The 2008 global financial meltdown erased $2 trillion in global wealth, froze credit markets, and delayed capital projects across industries[21]

Currency Volatility: In 2021, Turkey's lira lost 45 percent of its value, sending import costs soaring and forcing companies to renegotiate contracts[22]

Market Crashes: The Dot-Com Bubble of 2000 wiped out $1.7 trillion in market value, triggering budget cuts and layoffs throughout the tech sector[23]

Resource Shortages: The 2021 lumber shortage tripled prices, adding an average of $24,000 to the cost of a new US home[24]

Energy Crises: Europe's 2022 energy crunch pushed electricity costs up by as much as 500 percent for energy-intensive industries, forcing temporary plant closures.[25]

Economic shocks often leave leaders balancing competing priorities: conserving cash to preserve liquidity while still investing in capabilities needed for long-term competitiveness. Without a proactive plan, companies risk reacting too slowly, cutting too deeply, or missing strategic opportunities.

Strategic Response:

Financial Resilience: Post-2008, GE implemented continuous cash flow monitoring to ensure liquidity during periods of financial stress

Dynamic Pricing Models: Airlines use real-time algorithms to adjust ticket prices in response to fuel cost swings and demand changes

Energy Diversification: Toyota's solar-powered assembly plants in Japan help buffer against extreme energy price volatility.

Economic shocks test both the balance sheet and leadership discipline. The organizations that emerge stronger are those that have built flexibility into their financial models and decision-making processes long before the crisis arrives.

GLOBAL RESPONSE: FROM SHOCK TO STRENGTH

When a major disruption hits, the best-prepared organizations reposition themselves for long-term advantage. They do this because they understand that crisis management is not a one-size-fits-all exercise. The approach evolves as the situation moves from chaos to control, and finally, to transformation.

A robust global response framework unfolds in three distinct phases: immediate response, short-term adaptation, and long-term transformation. Each phase requires a different mindset, tools, and operational cadence. The secret is knowing when to shift gears.

Phase 1:
Immediate Response

The opening moments of a disruption are about preserving stability at all costs. At this stage, speed, clarity, and execution matter most. Your goal is to protect critical operations, maintain confidence among stakeholders, and buy enough time to make informed decisions.

The first actions you take can set the tone for the entire crisis. Ford's swift pivot during COVID-19, repurposing assembly lines to produce ventilators within weeks, demonstrated how decisive leadership can turn urgency into tangible results. Similarly, Maersk's real-time customer updates during the 2021 shipping delays didn't solve the backlog, but they did keep customers informed and confident.

Core Actions:

Activate crisis leadership: Predefined teams with clear authority can move faster than ad hoc committees

Establish clear communications: Keep messages concise, factual, and frequent to reduce uncertainty

Reallocate resources: Shift assets—whether trucks, talent, or inventory—to where they're most urgently needed

Engage emergency sourcing: Quickly identify backup suppliers for critical components to prevent production stoppages

Manage stakeholder confidence: Transparent updates maintain trust even when the news isn't good.

The aim in this phase is not to fix everything but to stop things from getting worse.

Phase 2:
Short-Term Adaptation

Once the immediate shock has been absorbed, the challenge becomes operating in a disrupted environment. Supply routes may be blocked, demand may shift unpredictably, and costs may spike. At this stage, agility is your most valuable capability.

This is when organizations prove whether they can adapt their playbook in real time. During the Suez Canal blockage in 2021, companies rerouted shipments around the Cape of Good Hope, expensive but one that kept goods moving. Amazon, faced with pandemic-driven delays, shifted inventory closer to customers in urban hubs to shorten delivery times.

Core Actions:

Reroute supply flows: Find and use alternative transport corridors to bypass bottlenecks

Rebalance inventory: Position stock where it will have the most immediate impact

Expand sourcing temporarily: Bring in supplementary suppliers to fill urgent gaps

Prioritize strategically: Focus on the customers, markets, and products that protect your margins and relationships

Control costs surgically: Make cuts that preserve capability without undermining future competitiveness.

Adaptation is about flexibility without losing focus. The companies that excel here protect their core business while positioning for recovery.

Phase 3:
Long-Term Transformation

A crisis is never just an interruption; it's also an audit of your business model. When the dust settles, the best organizations use the disruption as a catalyst for transformation.

Long-term resilience means diversifying your network, strengthening your partnerships, and embedding flexibility into operations. After the 2011 Tōhoku earthquake, Apple restructured production to avoid heavy concentration in any one country.

Core Actions:

Redesign networks: Spread risk across geographies and suppliers to avoid overexposure

Embed risk management: Use stress tests and scenario planning to identify vulnerabilities in advance

Build resilience into operations: Incorporate buffer stocks, flexible manufacturing, and redundant capabilities

Deepen partnerships: Develop collaborative relationships that share both risks and rewards

Adopt enabling technology: Leverage AI, blockchain, and IoT for real-time visibility and faster decision-making

Reassess operational models: Consider nearshoring or local production to improve speed and reduce risk.

The transformation phase isn't about returning to where you were but about creating a new, stronger normal. The disruptions you've weathered should make your organization faster, more adaptable, and better aligned with future realities.

Crisis management is a continuum, not a checklist. Organizations that act decisively in the moment, adapt intelligently as conditions evolve, and treat every disruption as an opportunity build lasting capability. In a world where global shocks are a certainty, resilience isn't a department, it's a culture.

MODERN TOOLS FOR GLOBAL CHALLENGES

Responding to disruption is about having the right data, technology, and insight at your fingertips before the crisis hits. Modern value chains move too fast, and disruptions spread too far, for reaction alone to be enough. Successful organizations are those that monitor early, model often, and act with precision.

While every company's tool kit will differ, the most resilient share three core capabilities: risk monitoring, scenario planning, and technology integration. Together, these create an operating environment where decisions can be made in hours instead of weeks, and actions can be taken before small problems become headline events.

Risk Monitoring: Seeing Trouble Before It Sees You

Visibility is the first line of defense in a volatile world. The earlier you detect a disruption—whether it's political unrest, a supplier's financial trouble, or an incoming hurricane—the more options you have to respond.

Modern risk monitoring systems bring together global event tracking, supplier performance surveillance, market intelligence, weather forecasting, and political risk assessment into a single decision-support framework. Some of my favorite tools are:

Everstream Analytics delivers real-time alerts on natural disasters, labor actions, and geopolitical shifts, giving companies precious lead time to adjust operations

Resilinc maps supplier networks down to the second and third tiers, flagging vulnerabilities from natural disaster exposure to political instability

IBM's Weather Company integrates forecasts into supply chain platforms so shipments can be rerouted before a storm hits

Verisk Maplecroft provides geopolitical risk scoring to anticipate instability before it disrupts operations.

Risk monitoring is about having clear visibility across your value chain so you can act early, turning potential crises into manageable events.

Scenario Planning: Turning "What If" into "What's Next"

The second capability is the ability to rehearse disruption before it happens. Scenario planning prepares you to win no matter what version of the future shows up.

This process involves disruption modeling, response simulation, impact analysis, recovery planning, and capability assessment. Examples include:

- **RiskLens** allows companies to simulate the financial impact of specific disruptions, from port closures to currency devaluations.

- **Siemens** uses digital twins to stress-test entire supply networks, identifying potential choke points.

- **McKinsey's COVID-19 framework** helped companies forecast consumer behavior shifts and prepare for prolonged demand surges in certain categories.

- **Deloitte's readiness tools** assess operational resilience, highlighting where capability gaps would cause break-downs under stress.

Well-run scenario planning ensures you don't just have a response plan, but multiple plans, all tested, all resourced, and all ready to execute.

Technology Integration: Digital Tools for Physical Problems

Finally, technology is the backbone of modern resilience. Integrated systems allow organizations to detect, decide, and deploy responses faster than the disruption can spread.

Some of the most impactful technologies include:

- **AI Prediction:** Platforms like Blue Yonder use machine learning to forecast demand shifts, identify risks, and optimize inventory. Coca-Cola used AI to cut stockouts by 20 percent during the pandemic.[26]

- **Blockchain Tracking:** Maersk's TradeLens uses block-chain to provide a transparent, tamper-proof record of shipments, cutting customs processing times by up to 40 percent[27.]

- **IoT Monitoring:** DHL employs IoT sensors to track temperature, humidity, and shock in real time for sensitive cargo like pharmaceuticals.[28]

- **Digital Twins:** GE and Unilever use virtual models of supply networks to test process changes and optimize flows, saving millions in energy and operational costs.[29]

- **Automated Response Systems:** Platforms like Kinaxis automatically adjust procurement, production, and logistics plans in real time when a disruption is detected.[30]

Technology integration is about more than buying tools; it's also about designing an ecosystem where data flows seamlessly, decisions are informed instantly, and execution happens without delay.

Risk monitoring tells you what's coming. Scenario planning shows you what to do about it. Technology integration makes sure you can act—fast and at scale.

These aren't "nice to have" capabilities—they're the difference between a value chain that buckles under pressure and one that emerges stronger from each disruption. In a world where global shocks are inevitable, the real competitive advantage is not avoiding turbulence but navigating through it better than anyone else.

Modern tools give leaders the visibility, foresight, and agility to respond to disruption, but technology alone cannot save an organization. True resilience is structural. It is designed into the network, embedded in relationships, and reinforced by the way a business operates every single day. The most resilient value chains are not accidents but the result of deliberate decisions about where to operate, who to partner with, and how to integrate technology into the heartbeat of the enterprise. When these three elements work in unison, they form a system that can absorb shocks, adapt quickly, and continue delivering value despite the chaos.

In times of stress, partnerships can be a lifeline or a liability. The difference lies in the depth of the relationship, long before a crisis hits. True partnerships go beyond transactional exchanges to become mutual commitments. Intel's approach during the semiconductor shortage, prioritizing long-standing partners, secured critical supplies ahead of competitors. Unilever's practice of sharing forecasts and demand signals with major retailers has helped smooth seasonal volatility and avoid costly stockouts. In some cases, cooperation extends across competitive lines, as seen when airlines pooled resources to repatriate citizens during the early stages of COVID-19. Effective partnerships also reach into the public sector. Following the collapse of the Francis Scott Key bridge in 2024, public and private organizations worked together to reopen the Port of Baltimore in record time, minimizing the disruption to critical industries like automotive and manufacturing.

Resilience is not about avoiding shocks; it is about creating systems that perform under pressure. A value chain designed for resilience can do more than survive a disruption—it can seize opportunities in the midst of it. When networks are diversified, partnerships are strong, and technology is deeply integrated, every disruption becomes less of a crisis and more of a stress test that the organization is prepared to pass. In today's world, that capability is not simply a competitive advantage—it is a prerequisite for long-term relevance.

THE FUTURE OF GLOBAL DISRUPTIONS

If the past decade has taught us anything, it is that global disruptions are no longer rare occurrences, they are the new operating environment. They arrive faster, ripple further, and interact in ways that make their impacts both unpredictable and prolonged. Understanding what's coming is no longer a matter of strategic foresight—it's an operational necessity.

Climate change will remain one of the most significant disruptors. Rising sea levels threaten port cities like Shanghai and Miami, while extreme weather events, from hurricanes and droughts to wildfires, increase in both frequency and severity. The costs are staggering; by 2050, climate-related damages could strip $23 trillion annually from the global economy. The physical risks are obvious, but the secondary effects, such as insurance market withdrawals, forced relocation of infrastructure, and shifting agricultural patterns, create knock-on disruptions throughout global value chains.[31]

Technology will drive both transformation and new vulnerabilities. Advances such as autonomous vehicles, quantum computing, and 3D printing promise to reconfigure production and logistics in ways that enhance efficiency and reduce dependency on certain geographies. But these same advances will open new avenues for cyberattacks, intellectual property theft, and ethical dilemmas over data use. As capabilities expand, so will the complexity of managing their risks.

Demographics will reshape both labor markets and consumption patterns. Aging populations in developed nations will tighten labor availability in manufacturing, transportation, and skilled trades, while youthful demographics in regions like Africa will create new markets and potential workforce hubs. The balance of global demand and supply will shift accordingly, and businesses that fail to anticipate these shifts may find themselves outpaced by more agile competitors.

Resource scarcity is another defining challenge. With demand for rare earth minerals, lithium, and cobalt soaring, competition for these inputs is already heightening geopolitical tensions. The race to secure supply will drive innovation in recycling and substitution, but it will also expose vulnerabilities for industries dependent on these finite resources. Water scarcity, projected to displace up to seven hundred million people by 2040, will compound these pressures, threatening stability in entire regions.[32]

Social change will alter the expectations placed on businesses. Consumers are increasingly demanding transparency, ethical sourcing, and genuine commitments to sustainability. These are no longer niche preferences; they are becoming mainstream market forces. Organizations that fail to integrate these into their value chains will face not only reputational risk but also potential loss of market share to more aligned competitors.

Meeting these emerging challenges requires more than adaptation—it demands the evolution of how we prepare and respond. Predictive capabilities powered by AI and machine learning will enable earlier detection of disruptions, giving organizations time to adapt before crises escalate. Response automation will streamline the execution of contingency plans, ensuring that operational pivots happen in hours rather than weeks. Building resilience will become a core business function, embedded in modular manufacturing, diversified sourcing, and rigorous stress-testing.

Collaboration will move from a strategic choice to a survival imperative. Multi-stakeholder partnerships, connecting businesses, governments, and NGOs, will be essential for addressing disruptions that transcend borders and industries. Just as important, sustainability will become inseparable from resilience. Circular economy models, renewable energy adoption, and waste minimization will not only protect the environment but also shield organizations from resource volatility and regulatory pressures.

Professionals are those who are prepared before disruption strikes. In a world where volatility is the baseline, building the capacity to anticipate, adapt, and align with emerging realities is the ultimate competitive advantage. The future will not wait for us to be ready, so readiness must be built into everything we do.

THE BOTTOM LINE:
FORTUNA FAVET PARATIS (FORTUNE FAVORS THE PREPARED)

Global disruptions are like the tides, inevitable, powerful, and beyond our control. From earthquakes to pandemics, trade wars to economic shocks, each event leaves behind a clear truth: Resilience is not an optional feature of a value chain, it is its defining characteristic. The organizations that prevail are those that treat resilience as a continuous capability, not a crisis-driven reaction.

Value chains today face challenges the Romans never could have imagined, but the solutions are rooted in the same principles: Plan for the long term, adapt to the unexpected, and build systems that last. The Romans didn't build aqueducts to handle a single rainy season; they built for centuries of use. We need to think the same way.

Preparedness is no longer about stockpiling resources or drafting contingency binders that gather dust. It is about designing networks that can flex under pressure, building partnerships that deliver mutual support when conditions deteriorate, and integrating technology that provides visibility, predictive insight, and the ability to act in real time. More than a defensive strategy, it is a foundation for opportunity, because disruptions often create as many openings as they close.

The leaders who will define the next decade understand that global events reveal their organization's strengths and weaknesses. They recognize that speed matters, but foresight matters more. And they know that in an interconnected world, no value chain stands alone; resilience is built through alignment with partners, communities, and even competitors.

History reminds us that every disruption eventually passes. The question is what remains when it does. For those who have built resilience into the core of their value chain, the answer is simple: stronger networks, deeper trust, and a sharper competitive edge. For everyone else, the cost of unpreparedness will be paid in lost markets, diminished reputation, and opportunities that slip away.

Global disruptions are inevitable. Resilience means bouncing back stronger, and if your value chain can adapt, learn, and evolve, you won't merely survive the next storm, you'll lead through it.

CHAPTER 10

THE FUTURE OF VALUE CHAINS

Value chains have always been built in motion. Roman roads weren't just stone and mortar—they were strategy, infrastructure, and political will poured into a single system that connected an empire.[1] The Silk Road wasn't only trade—it was trust, risk-taking, and adaptation across thousands of miles.[2] The East India Company wasn't only commerce; it was influence, negotiation, and relentless execution at scale.[3]

Today's networks are no less ambitious. They simply move at the speed of data instead of camel caravans, and the stakes are measured in market share, GDP, and reputations rather than grain shipments or barrels of spices.

Two thousand years ago, the biggest supply chain headache in the known world was getting live sharks to the Colosseum. Somewhere in the Roman Empire, a *claviger* was squinting at a clay tablet, muttering, "Teeth intact? XL size? No substitutions?" Meanwhile, the captured sharks were halfway across the

Mediterranean, probably seasick, definitely cranky, and very likely plotting revenge.

Fast-forward to today and your headaches might look different—products stuck in customs, container ships parked diagonally in canals, or a last-minute regulatory update in a country you didn't even know you were operating in. The scale has changed. The technology has changed. The stakes have skyrocketed. But the truth remains: Someone still has to get the right thing to the right place at the right time, preferably without losing money, market share, or their mind.

From Roads to Algorithms: The Unbroken Thread

The value chain has always been a reflection of its time. Roman infrastructure, the Silk Road, and the East India Company, each was a technological marvel in its own right, optimized for the constraints and opportunities of its era.

Today's equivalent is less about the physical road and more about the digital infrastructure: ERP systems, AI forecasting models, autonomous freight networks, and blockchain ledgers that promise transparency down to the lettuce leaf—because nothing says "peace of mind" like knowing your romaine lettuce has had an honest journey.

The throughline is clear: Every generation inherits the same basic challenge—move goods, ideas, and services through uncertainty, and the leaders who triumph are those who combine operational discipline with strategic foresight.

The Pillars in Motion

Now, you've seen that the seven pillars aren't a checklist to tick once and forget. They're more like a ship's rigging: constantly adjusted, depending on the wind, the currents, and the occasional appearance of pirates—whether the literal seventeenth-century kind or the modern-day "cybersecurity breach" variety.

Tactics keep you afloat in the storm. When a supplier goes under or a shipment is delayed, your systems and processes are the life raft

Strategy ensures you're not just drifting—you're charting toward the market position you actually want

Negotiation makes sure you don't pay a king's ransom for the privilege

Partnerships allow you to share the load and expand your reach

Inflation management helps you weather the economic squalls without capsizing your margins

Measurement keeps you aligned, accountable, and resilient, ensuring decisions are anchored in facts, performance is transparent, and anomalies are caught.

Global events test whether your value chain is built for resilience or merely for efficiency on sunny days.

It's not that these pillars exist in isolation; it's that their power multiplies when they work together. The best-run value chains look less like separate departments and more like a living ecosystem.

Now, Then, and Next

History never really leaves us—it simply changes outfits.

Here's how the same challenges have echoed across centuries:

Then	Now	Next
Roman grain shortages from Egypt[4]	PPE shortages during COVID-19	Climate migration shifting global food supply
Pirates in the Strait of Malacca[5]	Ransomware and ERP breaches	Quantum-enabled supply chain hacking[6]
Silk Road caravan delays	Shipping container shortages at key terminals	AI-predicted demand spikes reshaping logistics overnight
East India Company monopoly control[7]	Mega-retailers dominating supplier terms	Digital marketplaces dictating price via algorithm

The technology changes, but the human stakes, and the need for prepared leadership, do not.

The Road Ahead

The future will not be tidy. Globalization is splintering and realigning at the same time. AI is rewriting not only how we forecast demand but also how we decide what *demand* even means. Climate pressures are redrawing manufacturing maps. Governments are rolling out regulations that make yesterday's compliance standards look quaint.

And yet within this mess lies massive opportunity.

People who will win in the next decade will be those who:

1. Think like strategists and act like tacticians. They know the five-year vision but can also make a decision before lunch.

2. See partnerships as growth engines, not merely cost-sharing arrangements.

3. Negotiate for value, not just price.

4. Treat governance, finance, fraud prevention, and risk as core leadership tools, not "necessary evils."

5. Adapt faster than any disruption can spread.

The rest? They'll still be arguing about whose fault it was that the container ship got stuck in the first place.

Emerging Trends That Will Reshape Value Chains

Sustainability as Survival

A "green badge" on an annual report is no longer a license to operate. Carbon accounting will be as standard as financial audits.[8] The ability to meet Scope 3 emissions reporting will become a competitive advantage, not just a compliance task.[9]

AI and the Judgment Gap

Machines will get better at spotting inefficiencies, predicting demand, and routing shipments, but they will still lack human judgment. Everyone will need to master the balance between automation speed and human discernment.

Geo-Economic Realignments

We will see new global trade corridors and shifting alliances. Supply hubs will emerge in regions previously overlooked. Being regionally agile will matter as much as being globally integrated.

The Resilience Premium

Customers, investors, and regulators will increasingly reward companies that can prove they're prepared for disruption. That means redundancy, diversification, and tested contingency plans will move from "cost centers" to "value drivers."

The Future Leader's Tool Kit

The next generation of value chain leaders will need to carry more than just technical skills. If that's you, here's your starter pack:

Resilience Engineering—Because your plan is only as good as its worst day

Decision Agility—Making the right call without all the data—because you'll never have all of it.

Strategic Storytelling—Turning supply chain decisions into boardroom priorities

Ethical Courage—Saying no when yes would be easier but wrong

Partnership Orchestration—Getting multiple stakeholders to row in the same direction

Risk Fluency—Reading risk profiles like others read profit-and-loss statements

Cultural Intelligence—Navigating global teams without stepping on land mines—literal or figurative

Continuous Curiosity—Staying ahead of technology, regulation, and market shifts.

The Human Factor

For all our tools, data, and predictive analytics, value chains are still human-made, human-run, and human-broken. It's still people who design the systems, make the calls, and occasionally send the wrong thing to the wrong place—in one legendary case, a full truckload of only left shoes.

Which means leadership, not technology, will always be the deciding factor. Discipline will outlast motivation. Culture will outpace process manuals. And trust, once broken, will take more than a signed contract to repair.

So yes, invest in AI. Automate what you can. Digitize where it makes sense. But also invest in your people, in their ability to think critically, make decisions under pressure, and lead when the script gets thrown out the window.

What History Teaches Us About the Future

History's great value chains didn't merely survive because they had better roads, faster ships, or well-fed camels. They thrived because their leaders understood timing, relationships, and leverage.

- Rome didn't dominate because its roads were straight, it did so because it controlled access to them.[10]

- The Silk Road didn't endure because it was long, it endured because it connected cultures in ways that outlasted any single empire.

- The East India Company didn't rule the seas with firepower alone, it also mastered the quieter weapons of risk diversification, information control, and contracts locked up tighter than a port at midnight.

Your future will be no different. The tools will change—the human imperatives will not.

Your Map, Your Call

You now hold the map, a framework designed not for sunny days but for storms. You've seen how each pillar supports the others, how history informs the present, and how the leaders who succeed are those who integrate tactical agility with strategic clarity.

Where you sail from here is up to you. You can use these insights to squeeze a few more basis points out of your next quarter—or you can use them to build a value chain so resilient, so adaptable, that it becomes your competitive edge for the next decade.

If history has taught us anything, it's that fortune favors the prepared and, occasionally, the funny. So, lead boldly. Negotiate wisely. Partner strategically. Measure honestly.

Because in value chains, as in empires, your future isn't decided by what happens to you. It's decided by how you respond, how you lead, and whether you can keep moving forward when everyone else is standing still.

The next disruption is already in motion. The question is: **Are you ready?**

Value chains are built by people with the vision to see change coming and the grit to act before it's comfortable. You have the chance to build something truly enduring: A value chain that bends with the world, never breaks, and leaves a legacy of resilience long after the current crisis has passed.

The future is moving faster than ever. Step into it. Shape it. Own it.

NOTES

Introduction

1   Kenneth W. Harl, *Coinage in the Roman Economy, 300 B.C. to A.D. 700* (Johns Hopkins University Press, 1996).

2   Valerie Hansen, *The Silk Road: A New History* (Oxford University Press, 2012).

3   William Dalrymple, *The Anarchy: The East India Company, Corporate Violence, and the Pillage of an Empire* (Bloomsbury, 2022).

Chapter 1

1   Peter Heather, *The Fall of the Roman Empire: A New History of Rome and the Barbarians* (Oxford University Press, 2005).

2   Geoffrey Rickman, *The Corn Supply of Ancient Rome* (Oxford University Press, 1980).

3   Marie D. Jackson et al., "Mechanical Resilience and Cementitious Processes in Imperial Roman Architectural Mortar," *Proceedings of the National Academy of Sciences* 111, no. 52 (2014): 18484–89.

4   Walter Scheidel, ed., *The Cambridge Companion to the Roman Economy* (Cambridge University Press, 2012).

5   Valerie Hansen, *The Silk Road: A New History* (Oxford University Press, 2012).

6   Xinru Liu, *The Silk Road in World History* (Oxford University Press, 2010).

7   Susan Whitfield, *Life Along the Silk Road* (University of California Press, 2001).

8   John Peter Wild, *Textiles in Archaeology*, Shire Archaeology (Shire Publications, 2008).

9   Thomas T. Allsen, *Culture and Conquest in Mongol Eurasia* (Cambridge University Press, 2001).

10 Dalrymple, *The Anarchy*.

11 P. J. Marshall, *Bengal: The British Bridgehead* (Cambridge University Press, 1987), 18.

12 Hamilton Wright and C. Ernest Fayle, *A History of Lloyd's and of Marine Insurance in Great Britain* (Macmillan, 1928).

13 H. V. Bowen, *The Business of Empire: The East India Company and Imperial Britain, 1756–1833* (Cambridge University Press, 2009).

14 Julia Lovell, *The Opium War: Drugs, Dreams and the Making of China* (Picador, 2011).

15 Lovell, *Opium War.*

16 Sachin Kamble et al., "A Blockchain Technology Adoption Model for Supply Chain Transparency," *International Journal of Production Research* 58, no. 7 (2020): 2140–62.

17 National Oceanic and Atmospheric Administration (NOAA), *U.S. Billion-Dollar Weather and Climate Disasters 1980–2024*, NOAA National Centers for Environmental Information, 2025, https://www.ncei.noaa.gov/access/billions/events.pdf.

18 European Environment Agency (EEA), *Economic Losses and Fatalities from Weather- and Climate-Related Extremes in Europe*, EEA report, 2025, https://www.eea.europa.eu/en/analysis/publications/economic-losses-from-climate-extremes.

19 Barbara Levick and Kenneth Wellesley, *Year of the Four Emperors* (Routledge, 2011).

20 Connor Perrett and Madison Hall, "How a Dredger and a Fleet of Tugboats Helped Free the *Ever Given* Ship from the Suez Canal," *Business Insider*, March 29, 2021, https://www.businessinsider.com/how-ever-given-ship-freed-suez-canal-2021-3.

Chapter 2

1 Raymond Chevallier, *Roman Roads* (University of California Press, 1976).

2 Accenture, *Technology Vision 2024* (Accenture, 2024), https://www.accenture.com/content/dam/accenture/final/accenture-com/document-2/Accenture-Tech-Vision-2024.pdf.

3 Deloitte Digital and Fifty-Five, *Milliseconds Make Millions* (2020), https://www.deloitte.com/content/dam/assets-zone2/ie/en/docs/services/consulting/2023/Milliseconds_Make_Millions_report.pdf.

4 International Federation of Robotics, *World Robotics 2024* (IFR, 2024), https://ifr.org/img/worldrobotics/Press_Conference_2024.pdf.

5 Prologis, *Prologis 2022–2023 ESG Report* (Prologis, 2023), https://prologis.getbynder.com/m/341c024f0b023afa/original/Prologis-2022-23-ESG-Report.pdf.

6 Siemens, *Readiness for Predictive Maintenance at Scale Report 2023* (Siemens AG, 2023), https://assets.new.siemens.com/siemens/assets/api/uuid:8ee59c19-1c37-4516-a290-2844096f1cff/Readiness-Report-2023_original.pdf.

7 Shigeo Shingo, *Zero Quality Control: Source Inspection and the Poka-Yoke System* (Productivity Press, 1986).

8 Federal Emergency Management Agency, "Office of National Continuity Programs," FEMA, updated November 27, 2024, https://www.fema.gov/about/offices/continuity.

9 International Organization for Standardization, *ISO 8000-51:2023(en) Data Quality—Part 51* (ISO, 2023), https://www.iso.org/obp/ui/en/#iso:std:iso:8000:-51:ed-1:v1:en.

10 William Dalrymple, *The Anarchy: The East India Company, Corporate Violence, and the Pillage of an Empire* (Bloomsbury, 2022).

Chapter 3

1 J. D. Verhoeven, A. H. Pendray, and W. E. Dauksch, "The Key Role of Impurities in Ancient Damascus Steel Blades," *JOM: The Journal of the Minerals, Metals & Materials Society* 50, no. 9 (1998): 58–64.

2 Tesla, "Tesla Gigafactory: Nevada," Tesla, updated 2025, https://www.tesla.com/giga-nevada.

3 Raymond Chevallier, *Roman Roads* (University of California Press, 1976).

4 Dharmesh Mehta, *"Fulfillment by Amazon: How Improving Delivery Fueled Independent Seller Growth and Success,"* Amazon, September 24, 2023, https://www.aboutamazon.com/news/small-business/fulfillment-by-amazon-how-improving-delivery-fueled-independent-seller-growth-and-success.

5 William Dalrymple, *The Anarchy: The East India Company, Corporate Violence, and the Pillage of an Empire* (Bloomsbury Publishing, 2022).

6 United Nations Conference on Trade and Development, *COVID-19 and Maritime Transport: Impact and Responses* (UNCTD, 2021), https://unctad.org/system/files/official-document/dtltlbinf2020d1_en.pdf.

7 Accenture, *Technology Vision 2024* (Accenture, 2024), https://www.accenture.com/content/dam/accenture/final/accenture-com/document-2/Accenture-Tech-Vision-2024.pdf

8 A. P. Moller-Maersk, "Maersk's Digital Transformation," Maersk.com, accessed September 1, 2025, https://www.maersk.com/insights/logistics-trend-map/digital-transformation?exit=logistics-trend-map-report.

9   Procter and Gamble, *2023 Citizenship Report* (P&G, 2023), https://us.pg. com/citizenship-report-2023/.

10 Amazon, "10 Years of Amazon Robotics: How Robots Help Sort Packages, Move Product, and Improve Safety," Amazon, June 21, 2022, https:// www.aboutamazon.com/news/operations/10-years-of-amazon-robotics-how-robots-help-sort-packages-move-product-and-improve-safety.

11 Balu Chaturvedula, "Disrupting the Supply Chain Game—The Walmart Way," Walmart Global Tech, January 18, 2022, https://tech.walmart. com/content/walmart-global-tech/en_us/blog/post/disrupting-the-supply-chain-game-the-walmart-way.html; and Kasra Ferdows, Michael A. Lewis, and Jose A. D. Machuca, "Rapid-Fire Fulfillment," *Harvard Business Review*, November 2004, https://hbr.org/2004/11/rapid-fire-fulfillment.

12 Ferdows, Lewis, and Machuca, "Rapid-Fire Fulfillment."

13 Brad Stone, *The Everything Store: Jeff Bezos and the Age of Amazon* (Little, Brown, 2013).

14 Leander Kahney, *Tim Cook: The Genius Who Took Apple to the Next Level* (Portfolio, 2019).

15 Tesla, "Tesla and Panasonic Sign Agreement for Battery Production," Tesla, press release, July 2016, https://ir.tesla.com/press.

16 Ellen MacArthur Foundation, *Circular Economy Case Studies: IKEA and Unilever* (EMF, 2023), https://www.ellenmacarthurfoundation.org/topics/circular-economy-introduction/examples.

17 Semiconductor Industry Association, *2022 State of the U.S. Semiconductor Industry* (SIA, 2022), https://www.semiconductors.org/state-of-the-u-s-semiconductor-industry/.

18 Clayton M. Christensen et al., *Disruptive Innovation: An Intellectual History* (Harvard Business School Working Paper, 2015), https://www.hbs. edu/ris/Publication%20Files/McDonald_Rory_J07_Disruptive%20Innovation_a58c26e0-6f21-4197-9b34-c1ba3ed26c45.pdf.

19 James L. Watson, *Golden Arches East: McDonald's in East Asia* (Stanford University Press, 2006).

20 Jeffrey K. Liker, *The Toyota Way: 14 Management Principles from the World's Greatest Manufacturer* (McGraw-Hill, 2024).

21 Verhoeven, Pendray, and Dauksch, "Key Role of Impurities."

Chapter 4

1   William Dalrymple, *The Anarchy: The East India Company, Corporate Violence, and the Pillage of an Empire* (Bloomsbury, 2022).

2 John Keay, *The Honourable Company: A History of the English East India Company* (HarperCollins, 1991).

3 K. N. Chaudhuri, *The Trading World of Asia and the English East India Company, 1660–1760* (Cambridge University Press, 1978).

4 Nick Robins, *The Corporation That Changed the World: How the East India Company Shaped the Modern Multinational* (Pluto Press, 2012).

5 Dalrymple, *The Anarchy*.

6 Angus Maddison, *Contours of the World Economy, 1–2030 AD* (Oxford University Press, 2007).

7 IC Insights, "Global Semiconductor Industry Capital Spending Forecast," *IC Insights Market Report* (2021).

8 Stefano Aversa et al., "Automakers and Suppliers Need to Adopt 'All New Ways of Doing Business' to Master the Conversion to Electric Vehicles, Materials Shortages, the Rise of New Entrants and Other Disruptors Such as Autonomy and Connectivity, Says AlixPartners Analysis," press release, AlixPartners, June 17, 2021, https://www.alixpartners.com/newsroom/2021-alixpartners-global-automotive-outlook/.

9 Apple, *People and Environment in Our Supply Chain: 2021 Annual Progress Report* (Apple, 2021), https://www.apple.com/euro/supplier-responsibility/k/generic/pdf/Apple_SR_2021_Progress_Report_UK_IE.pdf.

10 IHS Markit, "Global Automotive Semiconductor Shortage Impact," S&P Global, 2021, https://www.spglobal.com/mobility/en/search/results.html?search=semiconductor+shortage+impact+2021.

11 Charles Fishman, *The Wal-Mart Effect: How the World's Most Powerful Company Really Works—and How It's Transforming the American Economy* (Penguin, 2006).

12 Port of Los Angeles, "2021 Port of Los Angeles Container Statistics," Port of Los Angeles, accessed September 1, 2025, https://www.portoflosangeles.org/business/statistics/container-statistics/historical-teu-statistics-2021.

13 Chaudhuri, *Trading World*.

14 Lisa M. Ellram, "Total Cost of Ownership: An Analysis Approach for Purchasing," *International Journal of Physical Distribution and Logistics Management* 25, no. 8 (1995): 4–23, https://doi.org/10.1108/09600039510099928.

15 Gartner Research, "How to Structure Penalties and Incentives for Managed Services Outsourcing Contracts," Gartner Research, August 9, 2021, https://www.gartner.com/en/documents/4004490.

16 Baker McKenzie, *COVID-19: Implications for the Future of Dispute Resolution* (Baker McKenzie, 2020), https://www.bakermckenzie.com/-/media/files/insight/publications/2020/04/covid19-implications-for-the-future-of-dispute-resolution_v5.pdf.

17 Albert Mehrabian, *Nonverbal Communication* (Aldine-Atherton, 1972).

18 P. J. Marshall, *The Making and Unmaking of Empires: Britain, India, and America, c. 1750–1783* (Oxford University Press, 2005).

19 McKinsey and Company, *The State of AI in 2023: Generative AI's Breakout Year* (McKinsey and Company, 2023), https://www.mckinsey.com/capabilities/quantumblack/our-insights/the-state-of-ai-in-2023-generative-ais-breakout-year.

20 Wood Mackenzie, *The Majors' Benchmarking 2022* (Wood Mackenzie, 2022), https://www.woodmac.com/reports/upstream-oil-and-gas-the-majors-benchmarking-2022-150049627/.

21 PricewaterhouseCoopers, *Supply Chain and Third Party Resilience During COVID-19 Disruption*, PwC, April 22, 2020, https://www.pwc.com/jg/en/issues/covid-19/pwc-supply-chain-resilience.pdf.

Chapter 5

1 John Keay, *The Honourable Company: A History of the English East India Company* (HarperCollins, 1991).

2 K. N. Chaudhuri, *The Trading World of Asia and the English East India Company, 1660–1760* (Cambridge University Press, 1978).

3 Tesla, *2023 Impact Report* (Tesla, 2023), https://www.tesla.com/ns_videos/2023-tesla-impact-report-highlights.pdf.

4 William Dalrymple, *The Anarchy: The East India Company, Corporate Violence, and the Pillage of an Empire* (Bloomsbury, 2022).

5 Stefano Aversa et al., "Automakers and Suppliers Need to Adopt 'All New Ways of Doing Business' to Master the Conversion to Electric Vehicles, Materials Shortages, the Rise of New Entrants and Other Disruptors Such as Autonomy and Connectivity, Says AlixPartners Analysis," press release, AlixPartners, June 17, 2021, https://www.alixpartners.com/newsroom/2021-alixpartners-global-automotive-outlook/.

6 Roger Fisher et al., *Getting to Yes: Negotiating Agreement Without Giving In*, 3rd ed. (Penguin, 2011).

7 Keay, *Honourable Company.*

8 Charles Fishman, *The Wal-Mart Effect: How the World's Most Powerful Company Really Works—and How It's Transforming the American Economy* (Penguin, 2006).

9   World Intellectual Property Organization, *World Intellectual Property Indicators 2022* (WIPO, 2022), https://www.wipo.int/edocs/pubdocs/en/wipo-pub-941-2022-en-world-intellectual-property-indicators-2022.pdf.

10 Brad Stone, *The Everything Store: Jeff Bezos and the Age of Amazon* (Little, Brown, 2013).

11 Dalrymple, *The Anarchy.*

12 Valerie Hansen, *The Silk Road: A New History* (Oxford University Press, 2012).

13 Peter Temin, *The Roman Market Economy* (Princeton University Press, 2013).

14 Dalrymple, *The Anarchy.*

15 Susan Whitfield, *Life Along the Silk Road* (University of California Press, 1999).

16 P. J. Marshall, *Bengal: The British Bridgehead* (Cambridge University Press, 1987).

17 Hansen, *Silk Road.*

18 Temin, *Roman Market Economy.*

19 Whitfield, *Life Along the Silk Road.*

20 Chaudhuri, *Trading World of Asia.*

21 Temin, *Roman Market Economy.*

22 Stone, *Everything Store.*

Chapter 6

1   Martin Goodman, *Roman and Jerusalem: The Clash of Ancient Civilizations* (Vintage, 2007).

2   Valerie Hansen, *The Silk Road: A New History* (Oxford University Press, 2012).

3   Peter Richardson, *Herod: King of the Jews and Friend of the Romans* (University of South Carolina Press, 1996).

4   Susan Whitfield, *Life Along the Silk Road* (University of California Press, 1999).

5   Xinru Liu, *The Silk Road in World History* (Oxford University Press, 2010).

6   William Dalrymple, *The Anarchy: The East India Company, Corporate Violence, and the Pillage of an Empire* (Bloomsbury, 2022).

7   P. J. Marshall, *Bengal: The British Bridgehead* (Cambridge University Press, 1987).

8   John Keay, *The Honourable Company: A History of the English East India Company* (HarperCollins, 1991).

9 E. R. Yescombe, *Public-Private Partnerships: Principles of Policy and Finance* (Butterworth-Heinemann, 2011).

10 Fergus Millar, *The Roman Near East, 31 BC–AD 337* (Harvard University Press, 1993)

Chapter 7

1 Richard Duncan-Jones, *Money and Government in the Roman Empire* (Cambridge University Press, 1994).

2 Roger Rees, *Diocletian and the Tetrarchy* (Edinburgh University Press, 2004).

3 Geoffrey Rickman, *The Corn Supply of Ancient Rome* (Oxford University Press, 1980).

4 Kyle Harper, *The Fate of Rome: Climate, Disease, and the End of an Empire* (Princeton University Press, 2017).

5 David Mattingly, *An Imperial Possession: Britain in the Roman Empire* (Penguin, 2006).

6 Cassius Dio, *Roman History*, trans. Earnest Cary (Harvard University Press, 1914–1917).

7 Rickman, *Corn Supply of Ancient Rome*.

8 "Global Chip Shortage to Cost Automakers $210b," The Stack, September 23, 2021, https://www.thestack.technology/global-semiconductor-shortage-automakers/.

9 Alison Futrell, *The Roman Games: A Sourcebook* (Blackwell Publishing, 2006).

10 Duncan-Jones, *Money and Government*.

11 Rickman, *Corn Supply of Ancient Rome*.

12 Analysis group, *Understanding Walmart's Impact on the US Economy and Communities, 2024* https://www.analysisgroup.com/globalassets/insights/publishing/2024_understanding_walmarts_impact_on_the_us_economy_and_communities.pdf

13 Mattingly, *An Imperial Possession: Britain in the Roman Empire, 54 BC - AD 409* Penguin Books, 2008)

14 Valerie Hansen, *The Silk Road: A New History* (Oxford University Press, 2012).

Chapter 8

1 Valerie Hansen, *The Silk Road: A New History* (Oxford University Press, 2012).

2 Jonathan P. Roth, *The Logistics of the Roman Army at War (264 BC–AD 235)* (Brill, 1999).

3 Kyle Harper, *The Fate of Rome: Climate, Disease, and the End of an Empire* (Princeton University Press, 2017).

4 William Dalrymple, *The Anarchy: The East India Company, Corporate Violence, and the Pillage of an Empire* (Bloomsbury, 2022).

5 Paul W. Ferris et al., *Marketing Metrics: The Definitive Guide to Measuring Marketing Performance* (Pearson Education, 2010).

6 Philip J. Stern, *The Company-State: Corporate Sovereignty and the Early Modern Foundations of the British Empire in India* (Oxford University Press, 2012).

7 Hansen, *Silk Road.*

8 Sanjay Subrahmanyam, *The Portuguese Empire in Asia, 1500–1700: A Political and Economic History* (Longman, 1993).

9 Fergus Millar, *The Emperor in the Roman World (31 BC–AD 337)* (Cornell University Press, 1992).

10 Dalrymple, *The Anarchy.*

11 Walter Scheidel, *Rome and China: Comparative Perspectives on Ancient World Empires* (Oxford University Press, 2009).

12 Hansen, *Silk Road.*

13 Robin A. Bryer, "Double-Entry Bookkeeping and the Birth of Capitalism: Accounting for the Commercial Revolution in Medieval Northern Italy," *Critical Perspectives on Accounting* 4, no. 2 (1993): 113–40, https://doi.org/10.1006/cpac.1993.1008.

Chapter 9

1 William Dalrymple, *The Anarchy: The East India Company, Corporate Violence, and the Pillage of an Empire* (Bloomsbury, 2022).

2 Amartya Sen, *Poverty and Famines: An Essay on Entitlement and Deprivation* (Clarendon Press, 1981).

3 Gallagher Research Centre, *The 2024 Noto Peninsula Earthquake* (Gallagher, 2025), https://www.ajg.com/gallagherre/-/media/files/gallagher/gallagherre/news-and-insights/2025/may/gallagherre-the-2024-noto-peninsula-earthquake.pdf.

4 NOAA, "Billion-Dollar Weather and Climate Disasters," August 9, 2025, https://www.ncei.noaa.gov/access/billions/.

5 AON, *Q3 Global Catastrophe Recap, October 2024*, https://assets.aon.com/-/media/files/aon/reports/2024/aon-q3-2024-global-catastrophe-recap.pdf.

6 Arnar Tomas, "Complete Guide to the 2024-2025 Sundhnukagigar Volcanic Eruptions," *Guide to Iceland, December 4, 2025,* https://guidetoiceland.is/best-of-iceland/complete-guide-to-the-2024-sylingarfell-volcanic-eruption.

7 NOAA, "Billion-Dollar Weather and Climate Disasters."

8 International Monetary Fund, *World Economic Outlook, October 2020: A Long and Difficult Ascent,* October 2020, https://www.imf.org/en/Publications/WEO/Issues/2020/09/30/world-economic-outlook-october-2020.

9 Jong-Wha Lee and Warwick McKibbin, "Globalization and Disease: The Case of SARS," *Asian Economic Papers* 3, no. 1 (2004): 113–31, https://doi.org/10.1162/1535351041747932.

10 CNN Staff, "Shipping Delays Are Back as China's Lockdowns Ripple Around the World," CTVNews, May 6, 2022, https://www.ctvnews.ca/business/article/shipping-delays-are-back-as-chinas-lockdowns-ripple-around-the-world/.

11 Diansheng Dong and Hayden Stewart, "Higher retail meat prices during COVID-19 pandemic negatively impacted U.S. households in 2020, *USDA Economic Research Service, May 12, 2022,"* https://www.ers.usda.gov/data-products/charts-of-note/chart-detail?chartId=103878#:~:text=Home-,Higher%20retail%20meat%20prices%20during%20COVID%2D19%20pandemic,impacted%20U.S.%20households%20in%202020&text=During%202020%2C%20U.S.%20households%20spent,co.

12 De Ann Davis, "UC Davis Report Reveals Economic Impact of November 2018 Romaine Outbreak", *Western Growers, October 19, 2021,* https://www.wga.com/news/uc-davis-report-reveals-economic-impact-of-november-2018-romaine-outbreak/.

13 Fabian Koh, "Singapore To Focus On Stockpiling Essential Medical, Healthcare Supplies Moving Forward: Mti Permanent Secretary," *Channel News Asia, March 14, 2023,* https://www.channelnewsasia.com/singapore/singapore-focus-stockpile-essential-medical-healthcare-supplies-ministry-of-trade-and-industry-permanent-secretary-3345421.

14 Chad P. Bown, *US-China Trade Tariffs: An Up-to-Date Chart* (Peterson Institute for International Economics, 2020), https://www.piie.com/research/piie-charts/2019/us-china-trade-war-tariffs-date-chart.

15 World Bank, *Global Economic Prospects* (World Bank, June 2022), https://thedocs.worldbank.org/en/doc/18ad707266f7740bce-

d755498ae0307a-0350012022/original/Global-Economic-Prospects-June-2022.pdf.

16 Swati Dhingra et al., "The Costs and Benefits of Leaving the EU: Trade Effects," *Economic Policy* 32, no. 92 (2017): 651–705, https://bipr.jhu.edu/BIPREXTRAMATERIALS/20171023.pdf.

17 European Commission, *The European Green Deal – Striving To Be The First Climate-Neutral Continent,* https://commission.europa.eu/strategy-and-policy/priorities-2019-2024/european-green-deal_en.

18 ResearchGate, "Brent Crude Spot Price", https://www.researchgate.net/figure/The-rise-of-oil-prices-following-the-Arab-Spring-event_fig1_291376469.

19 Nathan Jolly, "Michael Dell Says Customers Want Fewer Chinese Products," ANBOUND, April 21, 2023, https://www.anbound.com/Section/ArticleView_31784_13.htm.

20 Steven A. Altman and Caroline R. Bastian, "Special Update: Shifts in Global Business amid Trade Policy Turbulence," DHL, October 2025, https://www.dhl.com/global-en/microsites/core/global-connectedness/tracker.html.

21 International Monetary Fund, *World Economic Outlook* (IMF, April 2009), https://www.imf.org/en/Publications/WEO/Issues/2016/12/31/World-Economic-Outlook-April-2009-Crisis-and-Recovery-22575.

22 Ece Toksabay and Tuvan Gumrukcu, "Turkey's lira logs worst year in two decades under Erdogan", *Reuters, December 31, 2021,* https://www.reuters.com/markets/europe/turkeys-lira-weakens-fifth-day-monetary-policy-worries-2021-12-31/.

23 Eli Ofek and Matthew Richardson, "DotCom Mania: The Rise and Fall of Internet Stock Prices," *The Journal of Finance* 58, no. 3 (2003): 1113–37, https://www.nber.org/system/files/working_papers/w8630/w8630.pdf.

24 Outdoor Solutions, "Understanding the 2021 Lumber Shortage", https://outdoorsolutionsinc.biz/understanding-the-2021-lumber-shortage/.

25 Simone Emiliozzi, Fabrizio Ferriani, and Andrea Gazzani, "The Economic Consequences Of War – The European Energy Crisis And The Consequences For The Global Natural Gas Market", *VOX EU, January 11, 2024,* https://cepr.org/voxeu/columns/european-energy-crisis-and-consequences-global-natural-gas-market.

26 Irina Tumbovska, "AI Disrupts Logistics By Bringing Control To The Chaos", *SOLVEO,* https://www.solveo.co/post/ai-disrupts-logistics-by-bringing-control-to-the-chaos.

27 Thomas Jensen, Jonas Hedman, and Stefan Henningsson, "How Tradelens Delivers Business Value With Blockchain Technology", *MIS Quarterly* *18, no. 4 (December 2019): 221-43,*
https://www.researchgate.net/publication/345356583_How_TradeLens_
Delivers_Business_Value_With_Blockchain_Technology.

28 DHL, "The Real Value of Lot in Supply Chains," https://www.dhl.com/
global-en/delivered/innovation/the-value-of-iot-in-supply-chains.html.

29 "Digital and AI-Powered Supply Chain Productivity: Unilever's Perspective," *posted August 20, 2024, by Tredence, YouTube,* https://www.
youtube.com/watch?v=EUIqGcqEDdc.

30 Kinaxis, "Control Tower Capabilities For Transparency And Actionability," https://www.kinaxis.com/en/solutions/supply-chain-control-tower-and-visibility?attribution=mktg&campaignid=22297614660&adgroupi
d=176186313295&gad_source=1&gad_campaignid=22297614660&
gbraid=0AAAAA-qFxb3YXfmJRPzgQTmwlf4oWAvdT.

31 Swiss Re Institute, *The Economics of Climate Change: No Action* *Not an Option* (Swiss Re, April 2021), https://www.swissre.com/dam/
jcr:e73ee7c3-7f83-4c17-a2b8-8ef23a8d3312/swiss-re-institute-expertise-publication-economics-of-climate-change.pdf.

32 World Bank, *High and Dry: Climate Change, Water, and the Economy* (World Bank, 2016), https://www.worldbank.org/en/topic/water/publication/high-and-dry-climate-change-water-and-the-economy.

Chapter 10

1 Ray Laurence, *The Roads of Roman Italy: Mobility and Cultural Change* (Routledge, 1999).

2 Valerie Hansen, *The Silk Road: A New History* (Oxford University Press, 2012).

3 William Dalrymple, *The Anarchy: The East India Company, Corporate* *Violence, and the Pillage of an Empire* (Bloomsbury, 2022).

4 Geoffrey Rickman, *The Corn Supply of Ancient Rome* (Oxford University Press, 1980).

5 Martin N. Murphy, *Contemporary Piracy and Maritime Terrorism: The* *Threat to International Security* (Routledge, 2007).

6 National Academies of Sciences, Engineering, and Medicine, *Quantum* *Computing: Progress and Prospects* (National Academies Press, 2019),
https://nap.nationalacademies.org/read/25196/chapter/1.

7 Emily Erikson, *Between Monopoly and Free Trade: The English East* *India Company, 1600–1757* (Princeton University Press, 2014).

8 World Economic Forum, *Net-Zero Challenge: The Supply Chain Opportunity* (WEF, 2021), https://www.weforum.org/publications/net-zero-challenge-the-supply-chain-opportunity/.

9 CDP, *Engaging the Chain: Driving Speed and Scale* (CDP, 2022), https://cdn.cdp.net/cdp-production/cms/reports/documents/000/006/106/original/CDP_SC_Report_2021.pdf?1644513297.

10 Raymond Chevallier, *Roman Roads* (University of California Press, 1976).

ACKNOWLEDGMENTS

This book may have my name on the cover, but it was truly built on the support, wisdom, and encouragement of many people over many years.

To those who stood beside me, challenged me, and believed in this work before it ever made it to the page—thank you.

To Ann Given, who quite literally helped with everything, from research to edits to timely doses of encouragement—and comfort during more than one meltdown. Every author should be so lucky.

To Jennifer Santry, Rod MacInnes, Kevin Bergie, and David Campbell, your insights sharpened my thinking and helped shape key ideas that now run through every chapter. Thank you for being sounding boards, sparring partners, and champions.

To Mission Driven Press and Forefront Books, Isla Lake, and Jennifer Gingerich, thank you for your time, your red pens, and your belief in the power of this story to resonate. Your guidance made this book better in every way.

To Pam Johnson, Chika Daniels, Leela Aheer, Trey Humphreys, and Jonas Koffler, on the days when the words didn't come easily—or at all—your encouragement reminded me to keep going. You may not realize how much those nudges mattered—but they did.

To my darling sister Lindsay and my son Corbyn, thank you for your love, your patience, and for understanding when I disappeared into my writing cave again—and again, and again. You gave me the space and support to finish this.

To everyone who walked with me through the long arc of this journey, whether in person, on a call, or through the quiet encouragement of a shared goal, you helped make this real.

This book was written with grit, guided by curiosity, and finished with a whole lot of help from people who never let me forget why it mattered.

Thank you.

ABOUT THE AUTHOR

Stephanie Forbes is an internationally recognized expert in supply chain strategy, procurement governance, and operational resilience. With over two decades of experience spanning the energy, manufacturing, construction, and technology sectors, she is known for transforming complex global supply chains into agile, value-driven ecosystems. Stephanie is the founder and CEO of The Forbes Group, a boutique consultancy that helps organizations align people, processes, and systems to build competitive advantage.

Her leadership has been instrumental in shaping policy, driving sustainability initiatives, and advising boards and executive teams on fraud prevention, risk management, and performance measurement. She is also a keynote speaker on international stages, blending historical insights, modern practices, and humor to bring the world of supply chain to life.

In *Global Wealth, Local Impact: How Supply Chains Build Thriving Companies, Cultures, and Countries*, Stephanie invites readers on a practical yet visionary journey through time-tested strategies, real-world accounts, and future-forward thinking. Whether you're a CEO, a student, or a curious reader, this book is your playbook for mastering the value chain in an uncertain world.